The Willard Hotel

An Illustrated History

by
Richard Wallace Carr and Marie Pinak Carr

Color Photography by Carol M. Highsmith

DICMAR PUBLISHING ▪ WASHINGTON, D.C.

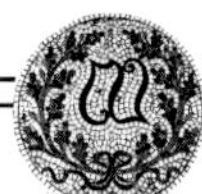

Book Design: Bonnie A. Burroughs
Color Separations: S&S Graphics, Rockville, Maryland.
Photographic Services: Carol M. Highsmith
Printed in China.

Any inquiries should be directed to the publisher.

ISBN: 0-933165-05-6

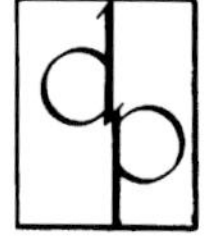

Dicmar Publishing
4057 Highwood Court, NW
Washington, DC 20007
(202) 342-0145

This book is dedicated to
our daughters Kate and Ann
and to all the people in whose heart
there is a special place for the Willard.

ACKNOWLEGEMENTS

While researching this book, we received encouragement and assistance of many organizations especially the Columbia Historical Society, the Kiplinger Washington Collection, the Washingtoniana Collection at the Martin Luther King Memorial Library, the Manuscript Division and the Prints and Photographs Division of the Library of Congress, the National Geographic Society and the Smithsonian Institution.

Editorial assistance has been graciously contributed by Mr. Hugh Lynch, Jr. and Mr. Kermit Roosevelt, Jr. Special thanks for the color photographic work goes to Mr. Neal Greentree with the assistance of David Patterson and to C.B. who typed and typed and typed.

CONTENTS

Carol M. Highsmith

AN INTRODUCTION TO ITS HISTORY

There is something special about the Willard, an affection born not so much of architecture, as from the knowledge that this place has been a stopping point for those who make history. It is a rare occasion when a building survives the ravages of time and the human tide to bear witness to the growth of a nation. It is rarer still that such a building should fade to the brink of destruction only to be saved by public affection, then to return to its grandeur and its place at the center of the Washington scene. Today, the Willard seems to glow with the beauty of a careful restoration and the stirring of seven score years of history.

Whether the footsteps of Lincoln, words of Whitman, memories of having to speak French to the waiters or the last dance of a high school prom, the Willard occupies a place in history as well as a special place in the hearts of those who have shared in those times. An elegant setting, attentive service, luxurious quarters and excellent food makes a hotel grand and provides the setting for memories large and small. There has been a hotel at the corner of Fourteenth Street and Pennsylvania Avenue since 1818. Since 1847, it has played a special role in the lives of the heirs of the Willard family legacy and, since 1901, the present structure has anchored the hotel in history.

From humble beginnings, the Willard has once again become a grand hotel on a grand scale. This book tells the Willard tale, chronicling its growth and development, good times and hard times, showing why it holds a special place in our past, and how the stage has been set for another one hundred and forty years. Hopefully, these pages will recall fond memories and help provide the setting for new ones. The human pageant parades on; let us hope that the Willard will continue to be a familiar stop to those who pass this way.

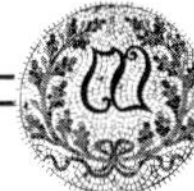

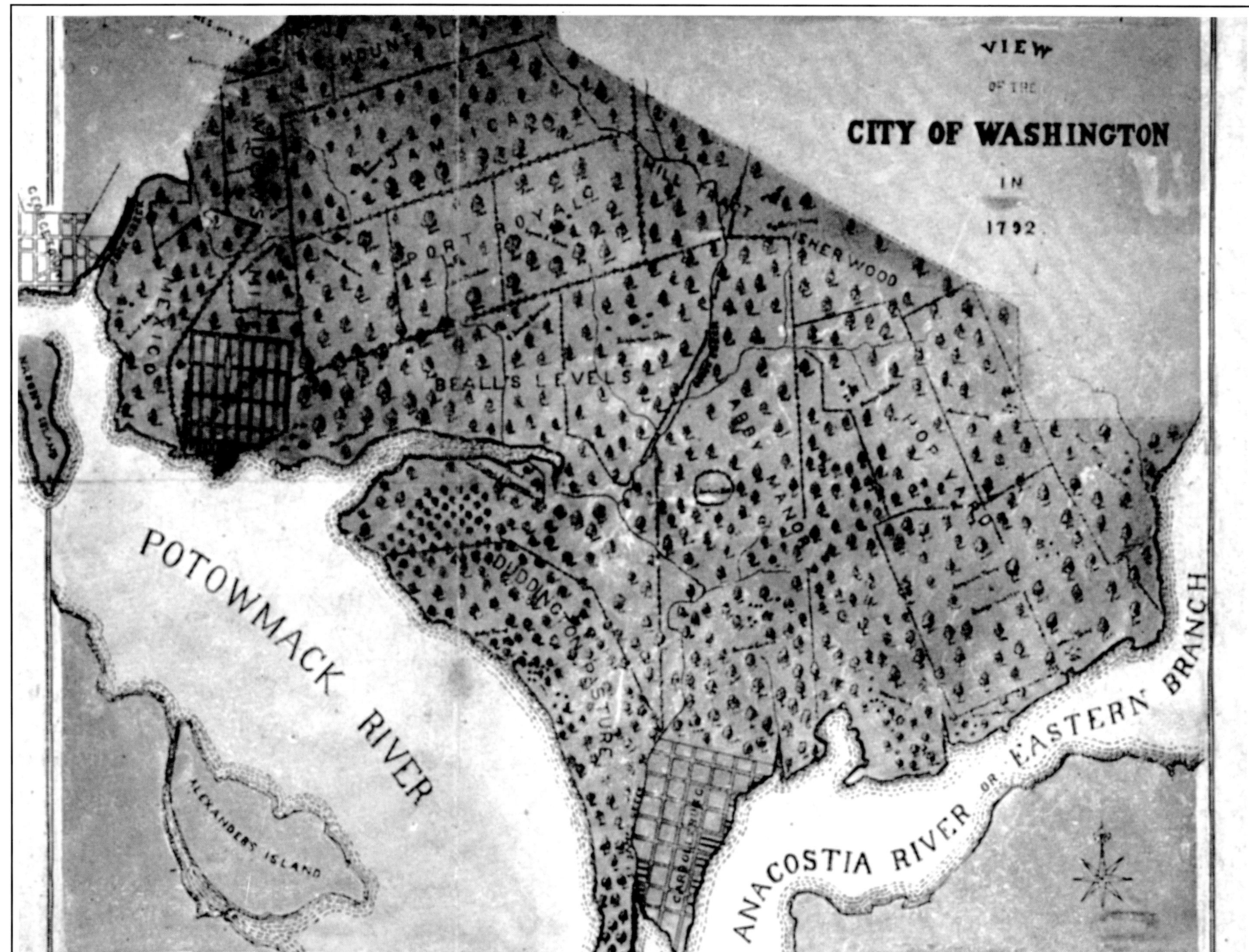

NCPC–Richard & Marie Carr Collection

Washington in 1792

Chapter I

A HOTEL ON THE AVENUE

Washington City was born of grand plans and modest beginnings. It became home to the national government, and as the first public buildings grew out of the plans of L'Enfant, Washington and Jefferson, the private city struggled to come alive. At the heart of this City, Pennsylvania Avenue was conceived by L'Enfant as a grand mile connecting the President's house with Congress, but in the early years after 1800, the avenue was more closely akin to a swamp than the boulevard of L'Enfant's dream. With time, improvements began and entrepreneurs took hold of this opportunity, however elusive, to meet the needs of our governing fathers. There developed various boarding houses, inns and hotels whose number grew as did Congress and the National government.

Capt. John Tayloe had been an early supporter of General Washington and his plans for the new city. His first enterprise in Washington was a town house known as the Octagon House. Tayloe's was a temporary residence for James and Dolly Madison after the British burned the White House in the War of 1812, and it is currently the headquarters of the American Institute of Architects. In 1816, Tayloe acquired the site on Pennsylvania Avenue at Fourteenth Street and built six two-story and attic dwellings as an investment. In 1818, the corner building was leased to Joshua Tennyson for a hotel, and from then on, but for rare intervals, there has been a hotel on that corner.

By 1822, the operation of Tennyson's property had passed to his partner, John Strother, who named it "The Mansion House". In 1824, Basil Williamson took over from Strother; later the hotel was operated by Frederick Barnard, then Azariah Fuller in 1833. Fuller opened under the name "The American House" which was later changed to "The City Hotel". Except for a brief period in 1836 when the buildings were leased to the government for the General Post Office, Fuller ran the hotel until 1847.

It seems that Fuller did not meet the expectations the owner or those of some of the guests. When Charles Dickens first visited this "City of Magnificent Intentions" in 1842, where he met with "poor eating houses, ploughed up roads, scorching hot mornings and freezing cold afternoons, all entirely out of everyone's way," he penned these memorable words about the City Hotel:

> *"The hotel in which we live is a long row of small houses fronting on the street, and opening at the back upon a common yard, in which hangs a great triangle. Whenever a servant is wanted, somebody beats on this triangle from one stroke up to seven, according to the number of the house in which his presence is required; and as all the servants are always being wanted, and none of them ever come, this enlivening engine is in full performance the whole day through. Clothes are drying in this same yard; female slaves, with cotton handkerchiefs twisted round their heads, are*

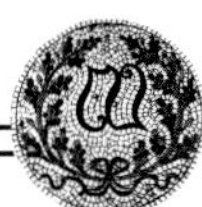

running to and fro on the hotel business; black waiters cross and recross with dishes in their hands; two great dogs are playing on a mound of loose bricks in the center of the little square, a pig is turning up his stomach to the sun and grunting 'That's comfortable!' and neither the men, nor the women, nor the dogs, nor the pig, nor any created creature takes the smallest notice of the triangle, which is tingling madly all the time."[1]

Kiplinger Washington Collection

Early Pennsylvania Avenue

Hotel accommodations in those early days were sparse. Sleeping quarters were frequently communal; sanitary conditions were in the early stages of development; and food was nourishing, but little more. For entertainment, there was the bar, meals, conversation, or a guest could attempt travel on Pennsylvania Avenue while perhaps dodging an occasional stray bullet from someone hunting in the marshes to the south. These were the times, and it was upon this stage that the Willards made their entrance.

Henry Augustus Willard was the first of the Willard family to come to Washington to go into the hotel business. Over the course of fourteen years, he was joined by four brothers who helped him run the hotel in varying ways and for varying lengths of time—Edwin Dorr Willard, Joseph Clapp Willard, Cyprian Stevens Willard and Caleb Clapp Willard. Cyprian S. Willard returned to his hometown of Westminster to be a farmer after a stay, presumed brief, of which little is written. Edwin D. Willard was the first to join Henry. He stayed just three years. Caleb C. Willard clerked in the hotel while a student, then went on to make quite a name for himself in Washington. Joseph C. Willard joined Henry a few years after business opened, and his heirs have ended up continuing the family tradition of involvement with the Willard even til this day.

Born in Westminster, Vermont in 1822, Henry Willard was an enterprising young man. After an unhappy experience clerking in a store, he got a job as a night clerk in Chase's Hotel in Brattleboro, Vermont. At that same time, Joseph Willard was clerking in a hotel in Troy, New York. Joseph recommended that Henry come to Troy, and both ended up being hired on the steamboat *Niagara* on the New York & Troy Hudson River Steamboat Line. Henry was steward, and developed a reputation for his ingenuity and service to his passengers. One of the jobs he undertook was described by his son:

"He was entrusted with the duty of carrying money from the banks in Troy to the banks in New York City, and I have often heard him say that when his boat would arrive late at night, it was a perilous and dangerous undertaking for him, a young man, to transport the money from the steamer to the banks. Not caring to keep the

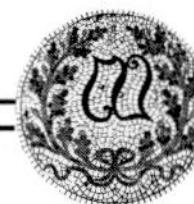

money in his state-room over night, he would often, when the boat arrived at a very late hour, go immediately to the banking house. At that hour of night, the clerks at the bank, who slept upstairs, would not come down and open the doors, not deeming it safe, but would, at a signal from him, let down a rope to the end of which a small pail was attached, and into this the packages of money and coin were deposited by my father; these would be pulled up by the clerk and taken into his window. My father was always very anxious that this money should be transported safely, and it can be said of him that not a dollar was lost. I can remember his saying once that he was, very late at night, walking up Broadway on his way to the St. Nicholas Hotel, when, out of a dark side-street, two thugs appeared a few feet behind him and called out: "Hello, young fellow, stop there!" He did not reply, but started to run as fast as he could, and he said that he ran so rapidly you could have put a dollar on his coat-tails, they stood out so straight. He sprinted so fast that he out-distanced his pursuers and reached the St. Nicholas Hotel safely; but his swift run up Broadway that night was one of terror."[2]

Another venture on shipboard that proved profitable for young Henry Willard was a library. He purchased currently popular books and other written pieces and lent them for a fee to the passengers to help them pass the time. This enterprise earned him nearly $2,000.00

It was this young, bright and attentive steward who Pheobe Warren recalled when she heard her fiance, Benjamin Ogle Tayloe, complaining of hotel problems. Phoebe Warren was the daughter of a wealthy Troy family and had traveled on a Willard-stewarded boat. Her fiance, had inherited the hotel property at Fourteenth Street and Pennsylvania Avenue from his father in 1822, but his recent managers had been permitting the hotel to run down, and the property was not as profitable as it should be. Mr. Tayloe met Henry Willard and, upon Ms. Warren's recommendation and his personal interview, offered Willard the job of running his City Hotel. With Tayloe's promise to invest in refurbishing the hotel, Henry Willard agreed, and he moved to Washington with the following announcement appearing in the *Daily National Intelligencer* on October 8, 1847:

Kiplinger Washington Collection

Jefferson Poplars on the Avenue

"Another New and Capacious hotel now presents itself to the view of the public, and challenges admiration, at the northwest corner of Fourteenth Street and Pennsylvania Avenue. This new City Hotel, just rebuilt and enlarged for the owner, B. Ogle Tayloe, Esq., will shortly be occupied by Mr. Willard, and ready for the reception of guests and visitors. The new City Hotel fronts 140 feet on Pennsylvania Avenue and 175 feet on Fourteenth Street. The main entrance to the building is by a large and handsome portico. There is also a private entrance from Pennsylvania avenue for ladies. The City Hotel contains about one hundred and

Kiplinger Washington Collection

Willard's City Hotel

fifty rooms, well arranged into sleeping rooms and suites of rooms for families. The ladies parlor is 22 feet by 32 feet, and opens upon a balcony on Pennsylvania Avenue. The gentleman's dining room is 94 feet long, 25 feet wide and 14 feet high. The ladies' dining room is 40 feet long, 27 feet wide and 14 feet high; it is easy of access from the ladies' parlor and all other ladies' rooms.

There are three large halls in the front building, 100 feet long by 14 feet wide, which will be well warmed by large coal stoves, so as to render them very comfortable in the coldest weather. They are all connected by two flights of broad stairs, with easy ascent, having oak rails and bannisters of superior workmanship, made by Mr. Harrod.

The kitchen, which is new fitted up by Mr. Nevett, is 94 feet long by 25 feet wide. It is conveniently arranged and supplied with the best culinary apparatus that can be had in this country. The hotel also contains a large wash-room, with a steam apparatus for washing and drying, also for heating water. There are also a large baking room, pastry room and ironing room.

The hotel contains a fine bathing room for ladies; another for gentlemen. Both of these bathrooms will be supplied with hot water from the steaming operations, and always ready for use.

We understand that the new City Hotel will be provided with entirely new furniture. It is expected the house will be opened about the 15th of next month."[3]

Early on, Henry Willard realized that he would need help in running the hotel. He wrote and asked his older brother Edwin to join him. Together, they both worked hard to make a name for their new enterprise. Recognizing the strategic location of their building between the White House and the Capitol, they strove to provide the best in hotel service and food in order to capture as much of the political business as

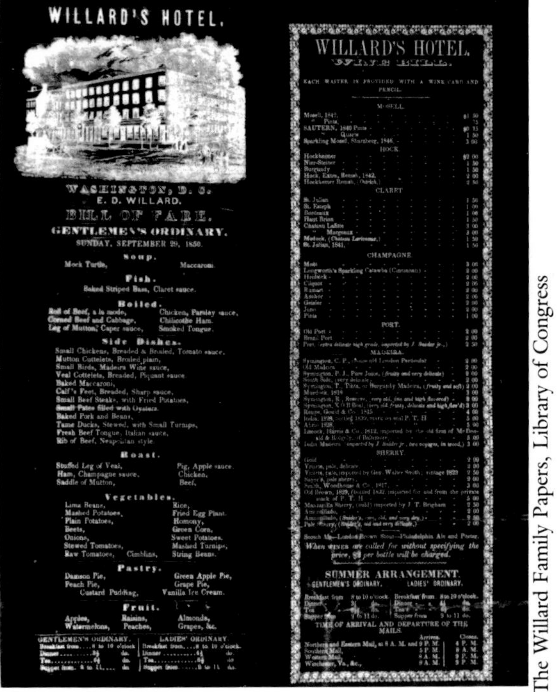

WILLARD'S HOTEL.

WASHINGTON, D. C.
E. D. WILLARD.
BILL OF FARE.
GENTLEMEN'S ORDINARY.
SUNDAY, SEPTEMBER 29, 1850.

Soup.
Mock Turtle, Maccaroni.

Fish.
Baked Striped Bass, Claret sauce.

Boiled.
Roll of Beef, a la mode, Chicken, Parsley sauce,
Corned Beef and Cabbage, Chilicothe Ham.
Leg of Mutton, Caper sauce, Smoked Tongue.

Side Dishes.
Small Chickens, Breaded & Broiled, Tomato sauce,
Mutton Cottelets, Broiled plain,
Small Birds, Madeira Wine sauce,
Veal Cottelets, Breaded, Piquant sauce.
Baked Maccaroni,
Calf's Feet, Breaded, Sharp sauce,
Small Beef Steaks, with Fried Potatoes,
Small Pates filled with Oysters.
Baked Pork and Beans,
Tame Ducks, Stewed, with Small Turnips,
Fresh Beef Tongue, Italian sauce,
Rib of Beef, Neapolitan style.

Roast.
Stuffed Leg of Veal, Pig, Apple sauce.
Ham, Champagne sauce, Chicken,
Saddle of Mutton, Beef.

Vegetables.
Lima Beans, Rice,
Mashed Potatoes, Fried Egg Plant.
Plain Potatoes, Homony,
Beets, Green Corn,
Onions, Sweet Potatoes.
Stewed Tomatoes, Mashed Turnips,
Raw Tomatoes, Cimblins, String Beans.

Pastry.
Damson Pie, Green Apple Pie,
Peach Pie, Grape Pie,
Custard Pudding, Vanilla Ice Cream.

Fruit.
Apples, Raisins, Almonds,
Watermelons, Peaches, Grapes, &c.

GENTLEMEN'S ORDINARY.		LADIES' ORDINARY.	
Breakfast from....8 to 10 o'clock		Breakfast from....8 to 10 o'clock.	
Dinner..........3½	do.	Dinner..........4½	do.
Tea..........6½	do.	Tea..........6½	do.
Supper from. 9 to 11....	do.	Supper from.....9 to 11	do.

WILLARD'S HOTEL.
WINE BILL.

EACH WAITER IS PROVIDED WITH A WINE CARD AND PENCIL.

MOSELL.

Mosell, 1842,	$1 50
" Pints,	75
SAUTERN, 1840 Pints	$0 75
" Quarts	1 50
Sparkling Mosell, Starzberg, 1846,	3 00

HOCK.

Hockheimer	$2 00
Nier-Steiner	1 50
Burgundy	1 50
Hock, Extra, Renish, 1842,	2 00
Hockheimer Renish, (Ostrich,)	2 50

CLARET.

St. Julian	1 50
St. Esteph	1 00
Bordeaux	1 00
Haut Brion	1 50
Chateau Lafitte	3 00
" Margeaux	3 00
Medock, (Chateau Larieuse,)	1 50
St. Julian, 1841,	1 50

CHAMPAGNE.

Moet	2 00
Longworth's Sparkling Catawba (Cincinnati)	2 00
Heidsick	2 00
Cliquot	2 00
Rumart	2 00
Anchor	2 00
Geisler	2 00
Juno	2 00
Pints	1 00

PORT.

Old Port	2 00
Brazil Port	2 00
Port, (extra delicate high grade, imported by J. Snyder jr.,)	2 50

MADEIRA.

Symington, C. P., [illegible] old London Particular	2 00
Old Madeira	2 00
Symington, P. J., Pure Juice, (fruity and very delicate)	[illegible]
South Side, (very delicate,)	2 00
Symington, T., Tinta, or Burgundy Madeira, (fruity and soft)	2 00
Murdock, 1819	[illegible]
Symington, R., Reserve, (very old, fine and high flavored)	[illegible]
Symington, X O B Bual, (very old, fruity, delicate and high flav'd)	3 00
Roupe, Gould & Co., 1815	4 00
India, 1828, bottled 1832, mark on seal P. T. H	5 00
[illegible] 1828,	5 00
Lamott, Harris & Co., 1812, imported by the old firm of McDonald & Ridgely, of Baltimore,	5 00
India Madeira (imported by J. Snider jr., two voyages, in wood,)	3 00

SHERRY.

Gold	2 00
Yriarte, pale, delicate	2 00
Yriarte, pale, imported by Gen. Walter Smith; vintage 1822	2 50
Sayer's, pale sherry,	2 00
Smith, Woodhouse & Co., 1817,	3 00
Old Brown, 1829, (bottled 1832, imported for and from the private stock of P. T. H	5 00
Mansanilla Sherry, (mild) imported by J. T. Brigham	2 50
Amontillado,	2 00
Amontillado, (Snider's, very old, and very dry,)	[illegible]
Pale Sherry, (Snider's, old and very delicate,)	2 00

Scotch Ale—London Brown Stout—Philadelphia Ale and Porter.

When WINES are called for without specifying the price, $[illegible] per bottle will be charged.

SUMMER ARRANGEMENT.

GENTLEMEN'S ORDINARY.		LADIES' ORDINARY.	
Breakfast from	8 to 10 o'clock.	Breakfast from	8 to 10 o'clock.
Dinner	3½ do.	Dinner	4½ do.
Tea	[illegible] do.	Tea	6½ do.
Supper from	9 to 11 do.	Supper from	9 to 11 do.

TIME OF ARRIVAL AND DEPARTURE OF THE MAILS.

	Arrives.	Closes.
Northern and Eastern Mail, at 8 A. M. and	9 P. M.	4 P. M.
Southern Mail,	5 P. M.	9 A. M.
Western Mail,	8 A. M.	9 P. M.
Winchester, Va., &c.,	8 A. M.	9 P. M.

The Willard Family Papers, Library of Congress

possible. During this time, the majority of Congressmen and Senators did not have private houses, but took rooms at hotels or boarding houses and a few well-known politicians did wonders for one's business. Evidence of their bounteous table is illustrated in a menu from 1850. Care was taken to see that the best food available was served and without waste:

"In those days, hotel keeping was very different from what it is now, and, at three o'clock almost every morning, my father would be called to go down to the Center Market, where he would personally buy his provisions and supplies for the hotel. Then, at the meal hours, especially at the dinner hour, my father presided over the carving table in the ante-room, and personally did the carving. In this way, he saw to it that no waste occurred."[4]

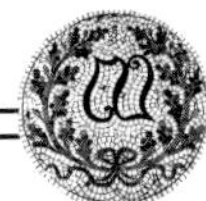

Surely, with this bill of fare, the patrons, as well as the table, must have groaned under the host's largesse.

Service met with success, and in 1850, the Willards remodeled the building again, tearing down the frame facade, building a new brick facade and enlarging the interior. It was also around this time that they first added the Willard name to that of City Hotel on the portico. Shortly thereafter, Edwin left the City Hotel to Henry and was involved in several other Washington businesses; management of the National Theatre, and management of the National Hotel on Pennsylvania Avenue at 9th Street, where he is credited with introducing the first gas stove in Washington which he designed and for which, in 1855, he made an application for patent.

During the next several years, Willard's City Hotel grew in reputation as one of the finer hotels in the City. It began to attract Congressmen and Senators as permanent guests as well as many of the prominent local businessmen. Henry even set his sights on the consummate politician, the President of the United States. In writing to Joseph Willard to ask him to come help run the hotel, Henry tells of his hopes of getting a presidential candidate, hopes which he would soon realize. Franklin Pierce won the election and moved to the Willard prior to being sworn in as President. The hotel had gained its first Presidential patron, an eye catching feather in its cap.

Henry succeeded in getting his brother Joseph to join him from California and Caleb from Vermont. Joseph had had a similar start in life to Henry. He had worked in a hotel in Troy, New York and then joined the staff of the steamer *Niagara* where be became Second Captain and enjoyed a reputation as popular as Henry's as evidenced from clippings from the *Albany Evening Journal* in 1846:

"Mr. Willard, the second captain of the boat, is known to all who have ever made the trip upon her, as a most attentive and gentlemanly officer, and it is not too much to say that his gentlemanly bearing and polite intentions, have contributed, in no small degree, to the popularity which the Niagara enjoys among travelers."[5]

Kiplinger Washington Collection

The Ebbit House

Joseph had gone to California to follow the gold rush but did not meet with success and finally traveled to Washington in late 1852. Caleb moved to Washington in 1849 where he attended school and worked in the hotel for four years. When he turned nineteen, his brothers gave him the management of the Hygia Hotel at Old Point Comfort, Virginia. Caleb left Washington until 1858 when he returned to help out at the Willard during an illness of his brother Joseph.

Caleb had no further association with the operation of the Willard, but he had an illustrious career. During the Civil War, he witnessed the battle between the *Monitor* and the *Merrimac*. In 1864, he returned to Washington to acquire the Ebbitt House which he improved to first class status, and he and his brothers shuffled customers back and forth across Fourteenth Street to each other when their respective hotels were full. President McKinley was a resident of the Ebbitt for fourteen years and became a good friend. Caleb eventually acquired a great deal of the real estate on F Street between Thirteenth and Fourteenth Streets including the Adams Building, and the Geological Survey Building, otherwise known as the Hoe Iron Building, and was a highly regarded member of the business community.

The early years also brought celebrities to the Willard doors. It was in Willard's that Henry Clay is reported to have mixed the first mint-julep served in Washington. In 1850, P.T. Barnum brought Jenny Lind, the Swedish Nightingale, to Washington, and they stayed at the Willard. They even held a levee for her admirers. Miss Lind's lovely voice was world renowned and cast a particular spell over one of her admirers in Washington, the much revered Daniel Webster:

> *"We are treated to another picture of him when he arrived late at a concert being given by Jenny Lind. For the benefit of the statesmen who were present, Miss Lind, for an encore, sang "Hail Columbia." Webster, who had been dining, was on his feet in an instant and added his powerful bass voice to hers in the chorus. Mrs. Webster did all she could to induce him to sit down, but he repeated his effort at the close of every verse, and with the last strain made the songstress a profound obesisance, waving his hat at the same time. Miss Lind curtsyed in return, Webster repeated his bow, and this little comedy of etiquette was kept up for some minutes, to the delight of the audience."*[6]

Richard & Marie Carr Collection

Jenny Lind

When she first came to town, President Fillmore called at the hotel and, Miss Lind being out, left his card. Upon her return, Miss Lind apparently wanted to call upon the President immediately but Barnum, explaining one of the virtues of the American Democracy, convinced her that it was not necessary, and they both enjoyed a private evening with the President and his family the following day.

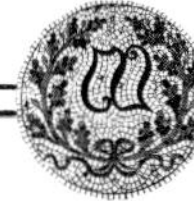

On November 23, 1853, Joseph and Henry Willard hosted a banquet to announce the reopening of their hotel with fanfare in the paper and flourishes at the table. In attendance were local notables such as W.W. Corcoran, Benjamin Ogle Tayloe, and Francis Dodge as well as members of the military and congress.

> *"On Wednesday evening, the Messrs., J.C. & H.A. Willard, the enterprising proprietors of the above Hotel, inaugurated its opening by a grand banquet, at which over one hundred guests sat down. It would be needless to mention that the bill of fare contained every delicacy, both in and out of season, that the wines were first rate, and the corps of the waiters indulging and attentive. Mr. C.C. Willard, the younger brother of the proprietors, who will attend to the office, was particularly conspicuous for the zeal and activity that he displayed on this occasion, appearing to be, if it were possible, in half a dozen places at once—the establishment, we sincerely believe, could not do without him."*[7]

The Honorable Edward Everett, former Secretary of State, was most generous in his comments about the Willards and the hotel that evening:

> *"I rose to speak of the Messrs.. Willard, but I am afraid I must speak for myself. Our friend Willard has made a slight mistake in saying that he did not like to make his own acknowledgments, and that I had kindly offered to speak for him, although it is most true that when requested to do so by my friend, (Mr. Tayloe) I readily consented. I do it with great cheerfulness, but if ever there was an occasion on which a man might speak for himself, it is on the present, and Mr. Willard need not distrust his ability to do so. There are occasions when deeds speak louder than words, and this is one. Instead of Mr. Willard returning thanks to us, it is we that are under obligation to him. In fact, I think, that in paying our respects to Mr. Willard, this evening, we are but doing a duty, though certainly a duty most easily performed. There are few duties in life that require less nerve than to come together, and eat a good dinner. There is very little self-denial in that. Indeed self-denial is not the principle which generally carries us to a Hotel, although it sometimes happens that we have to practice it, when there.*
>
> *To speak, however, seriously, it is not without some emotion that I find myself here. There are many interesting associations for me connected with this house. Under its roof, I have passed some of the happiest years of my life. Under the old regime, this building was divided into separate houses, and I was, with my family, the occupant of one of them for several successive seasons. Here, under its roof, at 500 miles from Boston, we were as comfortable as if at home, and I have no doubt that those who place themselves under your protection will find it so likewise. Under this roof I have had the honor and happiness, in company with my messmates, of entertaining at one and the same time, John Quincy Adams, Chief Justice Marshall, Judge Story, Mr. Calhoun, Mr. Clay, Mr. Webster. These are all gone, but together with them I can name another, now living, and not unworthy to be associated with them, Washington Irving.*
>
> *Think of men like these, six or seven of whom I have now named, gathered together at the same time around the festive board, under this roof. That was, indeed, the feast of reason, not merely the flashes of merriment which set the table in a roar, but that gushing out of convivial eloquence, that cheerful interchange of friendly feeling, in which the politician and partizan are forgotten. Yes gentlemen, there were giants in those days, giants in intellect, but in character and spirit they were gentlemen, and in their familiar intercourse with each other, they had all the tenderness of brethren."*[8]

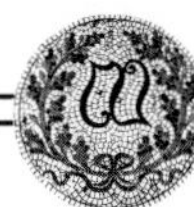

Kiplinger Washington Collection

Early Willard Hotel

After waxing poetic about his travels and his life in foreign inns, Mr. Everett closed with a toast touching off a cavalcade of further toasts, responses and warm comaraderie.

> *"The health of our friend Willard, and prosperity to his establishment; may it prove a benefit to the community, a house to the stranger, and a profitable enterprise to the proprietor."*[9]

The decade from 1850 to 1860 was a good one for the Willards. Their hotel business grew and was profitable, and the demand for the hotel increased so that the Willards began a program of expansion. After operating on a yearly basis for several years, on May 1, 1854, the Willards signed a ten-year lease with Benjamin Tayloe which included a purchase option, the source of a future controversy. In 1858, the Willards negotiated a ground lease with the Kearney family for their property, which extended up Fourteenth Street to F Street, for 99 years, also with an option to purchase. The last parcel related to the Willard Hotel was acquired from the First Presbyterian Church in 1859 when the First Presbyterian Church merged with the Second Presbyterian Church to form the new New York Avenue Presbyterian Church. As evidenced by its name, the Church was the first and oldest Presbyterian Church in the City and had been the place of worship of Presidents Harrison, Buchanan and Pierce. Originally built between 1807 and 1810, it was remodeled and expanded in 1832 and proved suitable for lectures, banquets, auctions, conventions and other entertainments for the hotel.

The Willards eventually purchased all of the land held under lease, and this they accomplished to their advantage. Henry Willard purchased one-half of the Kearney property on January 28, 1875 and Joseph Willard paid the balance of the second half on October 19, 1880. The Tayloe transaction, however, proved to be somewhat difficult. The Willards' lease with Tayloe provided that they could acquire the property at any time prior to the expiration of the lease for $22,500, payable $2,000 in cash and $20,500 in a note. On April 15, 1864, two weeks before the lease was to expire, the Willards sent by letter to Tayloe a check for $2,000, a receipt to be filled out and a proposal that the Willards would have the deed and the deed of trust prepared for execution prior to May 1. To this, Tayloe responded that he was presently busy but that he wanted to discuss the matter before he signed anything, and he returned the check. The following morning, Joseph Willard presented himself at Tayloe's doorstep with $2,000 in cash and requested that Tayloe proceed with the transaction, which Tayloe refused to do for two reasons. First, when the lease was originally signed, gold and silver were the predominant form of currency. By the time the Willards acted on their purchase option, Congress had made notes of the United States legal tender for debts. Unfortunately for Tayloe, as explained in the court records, one dollar in gold in April, 1864 was worth between $1.73 and $1.80 in United States bank notes. Second, Tayloe argued that the property was worth well in excess of the $22,500 sales price.

The Willards repeatedly delivered the money and drafts of the deed and deed of trust to Tayloe who, in turn, repeatedly returned them. Tayloe finally decided to leave town so that the Willards could not complete the purchase by May 1, the expiration of their lease. On April 29, 1864, realizing that Tayloe had fled to prevent consummation of the sale, Joseph Willard filed suit for specific performance setting forth the

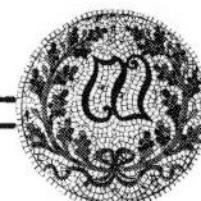

purchase option in the lease and his election to purchase. On January 24, 1870, the case was finally decided in the U.S. Supreme Court with a reasonably balanced decision. Tayloe had to sell the property to the Willards for the agreed price, and the Willards had to pay in gold and silver.

On a happier note, at the end of this first decade, The Willard was the setting for two grand events; the Napier Ball and the arrival of the Japanese Delegation to the United States. There was considerable intrigue relating to the ball stemming from President Buchanan's disapproval of the Napiers and Senator Steward's apparent intent to embarrass the administration, but a grand event was held, and the Ball was the talk of the town for many years. With elaborate presentation and a highly decorative menu, 1,200 notables were feted on February 17, 1859 from early evening until dawn:

> *"The grand social event of the Washington season came off on Thursday evening, to the general satisfaction of all concerned, as it was decidedly a highly successful affair, as a mark of the cordial respect and esteem to the two distinguished guests of the evening, it must of course have been highly gratifying to them, particularly as it was so perfectly free from sectional, political or local bias. There was no North, no South, no Republicanism, no Democracy in it, but, on the contrary, a cordial and a united feeling among all parties and sections of parties in doing honor to Lord and Lady Napier, and as a mark of the sincere regret at their approaching departure. So extended was this feeling that parties of ladies and gentlemen from Southern and Northern cities came to Washington for the express purpose of joining in the ovation; and though, until the supper room was opened, the crowd in the ballroom and ante-rooms was a little inconvenient, that very crowd only enhanced the*

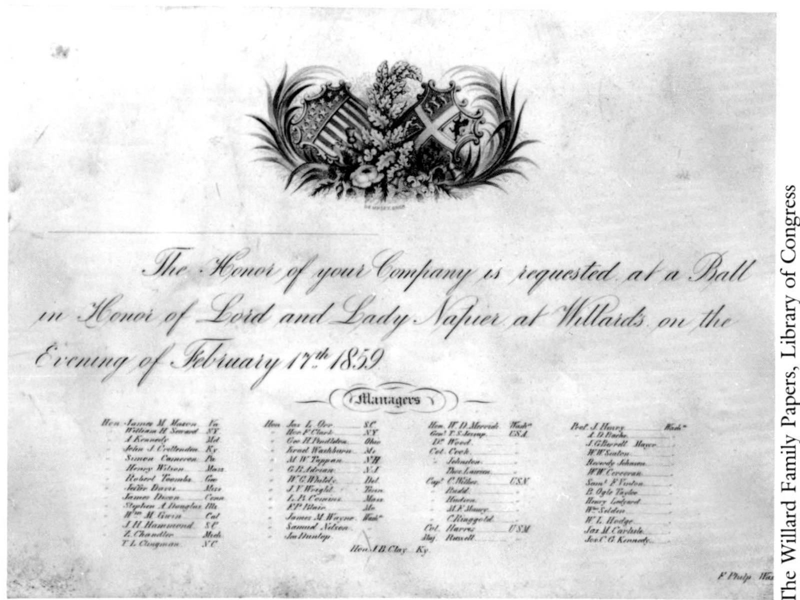

The Honor of your Company is requested at a Ball in Honor of Lord and Lady Napier at Willards on the Evening of February 17th 1859

Managers

Hon. James M. Mason, Va.; William H. Seward, N.Y.; A. Kennedy, Md.; John J. Crittenden, Ky.; Simon Cameron, Pa.; Henry Wilson, Mass.; Robert Toombs, Ga.; Jeffer Davis, Miss.; James Dixon, Conn.; Stephen A. Douglas, Ills.; Wm. M. Gwin, Cal.; J.H. Hammond, S.C.; Z. Chandler, Mich.; T.L. Clingman, N.C.

Hon. Jas. L. Orr, S.C.; Hon. F. Clark, N.Y.; Geo. H. Pendleton, Ohio; Israel Washburn, Me.; M.W. Tappan, N.H.; G.B. Adrain, N.J.; W.G. Whiteley, Del.; J.V. Wright, Tenn.; L.B. Comins, Mass.; F.P. Blair, Mo.; James M. Wayne, Wash.; Samuel Nelson; Jas. Dunlop

Hon. W.D. Merrick, Wash.; Genl. T.S. Jesup, U.S.A.; Dr. Wood; Col. Cook; Johnston; Thos. Lawson; Capt. C. Wilkes, U.S.N.; Rudd; Hudson; M.F. Maury; C. Ringgold; Col. Harris, U.S.M.; Maj. Russell

Prof. J. Henry, Wash.; A.D. Bache; J.G. Berrett, Mayor; W.W. Seaton; Reverdy Johnson; W.W. Corcoran; Saml. F. Vinton; B. Ogle Tayloe; Henry Ledyard; Wm. Selden; W.L. Hodge; Jas. M. Carlisle; Jos. C.G. Kennedy

Hon. J.B. Clay, Ky.

F. Philp, Was

Napier Ball Invitation

The Willard Family Papers, Library of Congress

> *value of the compliment. It was estimated that from twelve to fourteen hundred persons were present.*
>
> *At half past ten o'clock, Lady Napier, escorted by General Cass, the venerable Secretary of State, descended the broad stairway that landed in the ballroom, followed immediately by Lord Napier escorting the Lady of Judge*

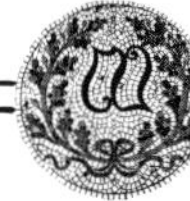

Wayne, and after them members of the Cabinet and diplomatic corps, each escorting a lady. On Lady Napier's appearance the full orchestra struck up the national anthem of Great Britain, followed by the national air of the United States.

The ballroom, which was one hundred and fifty feet long, was draped throughout its whole length with flags of different nations in a most graceful and beautiful manner, the stars and stripes with the red cross of England being entwined together. On the wall, opposite the broad stairs and immediately before them on the floor, the Napier arms were beautifully traced on a very large scale, the two knights that are supporters being of the size of life. Other parts of the floor had beautiful devices executed in artistic style. Over the two flags was a large device, very handsomely executed, containing the shields of Great Britain and the United States happily blended together, with the rose, shamrock and thistle on the former, and ornamented with the Indian cornstalk and leaves for the latter.

One end of the ballroom was occupied by a raised platform, covered with scarlet cloth, to which Lady Napier and the other distinguished lady guests were conducted, and where all who desired it were presented to her.

At the northern end of the room was a platform for the guests of the night, above which were full length portraits of Gen. Washington and Queen Victoria.

The whole scene was very brilliant, and we do not believe that there was ever before in Washington such a collection of beautiful women, a greater display of superb and costly toilet, or a more distinguished company, embracing as it did the high officials of the Government, Judges of the Supreme Court, the Speaker of the House of Representatives, members of the Foreign Legations, Senators and Representatives, Officers of the Army and Navy, and distinguished citizens, not only of the City, but from almost every section of the country, with the ladies of their respective families.

Between eleven and twelve o'clock the intervening curtain between the ball and supper room was raised, and the whole extent of the room, two hundred and seventy feet long, was then seen. At the upper end of the supper room a table forming three sides of a square was prepared expressly for the invited guests.

Lady Napier was handed to the table by the Hon. J.M. Mason, the Chairman of the Committee on Foreign Relations of the Senate, and also Chairman of the Managers—Lady N. with Mr. Speaker Orr on her right, being seated on the right of Mr. Mason, and Lord, who escored Mme. de Sartiges to the table, on his left other members of the Foreign Legations and of the Cabinet, with ladies, being all properly arranged in their respective seats.

The table was very complete in every respect, and did great credit to the Messrs. Willard for the variety, excellence, and beauty of the viands, confectionaries, ornaments, and general arrangement. Immediately in front of Lady Napier stood a pyramid of confectionary six feet high, with appropriate devices, and ornamented at the top with the figure of Britannia; and another similar ornament, at a different part of the table, emblematical of the United States.

The company did full honor to the supper, and though three to four hundred were able to be in the supper room at one time, it was kept constantly full until the wee hours of the morning, which is not at all surprising, under the temptations afforded by the abundant, varied and well-arranged bill of fare.

The music was excellent, consisting of a very able band of more than twenty instruments.

After two o'clock the company thinned off, but dancing was kept up to a later hour, with much spirit and apparent enjoyment."[10]

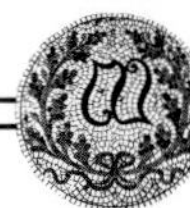

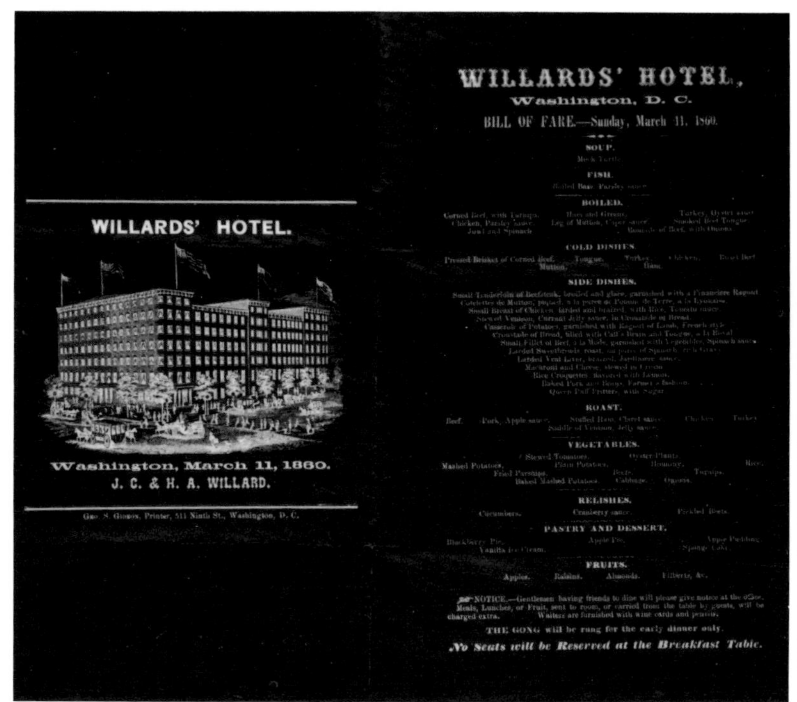

WILLARDS' HOTEL.

Washington, March 11, 1860.
J. C. & H. A. WILLARD.

WILLARDS' HOTEL,
Washington, D. C.
BILL OF FARE.—Sunday, March 11, 1860.

SOUP.
Mock Turtle.

FISH.
Boiled Bass, Parsley sauce.

BOILED.
Corned Beef, with Turnips. Ham and Greens. Turkey, Oyster sauce.
Chicken, Parsley sauce. Leg of Mutton, Caper sauce. Smoked Beef Tongue.
Jowl and Spinach.

COLD DISHES.
Pressed Brisket of Corned Beef. Tongue. Turkey. Chicken. Roast Beef.
Mutton. Ham.

SIDE DISHES.
Macaroni and Cheese, stewed in Cream.
Rice Croquettes, flavored with Lemon.
Baked Pork and Beans, Farmer's fashion.

ROAST.
Beef. Pork, Apple sauce. Stuffed Ham, Claret sauce. Chicken. Turkey.
Saddle of Venison, Jelly sauce.

VEGETABLES.
Stewed Tomatoes. Oyster Plants.
Mashed Potatoes. Plain Potatoes. Hominy. Rice.
Fried Parsnips. Beets. Turnips.
Baked Mashed Potatoes. Cabbage. Onions.

RELISHES.
Cucumbers. Cranberry sauce. Pickled Beets.

PASTRY AND DESSERT.
Blackberry Pie. Apple Pie. Apple Pudding.
Vanilla Ice Cream. Sponge Cake.

FRUITS.
Apples. Raisins. Almonds. Filberts, &c.

NOTICE.—Gentlemen having friends to dine will please give notice at the office. Meals, Lunches, or Fruit, sent to room, or carried from the table by guests, will be charged extra. Waiters are furnished with wine cards and pencils.

THE GONG will be rung for the early dinner only.

No Seats will be Reserved at the Breakfast Table.

The Willard Family Papers, Library of Congress

Bill of Fare–1860

With the acquisition of Willard Hall, the Willards were able to greatly expand the cultural events which they sponsored for the hotel guests and for the City. March, 1859 finds an extensive list of sponsors for a series of concerts by the beautiful Italian singer, Adelina Patti. Newspapers of those times include ads for such performances as The Mendelson Quintet Club of Boston, the Choir of St. Paul's Lutheran Church and a presentation by Mr. Walter S. Hunter on the "Isles and Shores of Africa".

Finally, in 1860, The Willard was selected to house the first Japanese Delegation to the United States. On July 8, 1853, Commodore Perry had sailed his fleet into Yedo Bay on a good will mission to establish relations with Japan. Perry's visit led to the preparation of a treaty which was signed by the Japanese and brought to the United States for ratification in May of 1860. The Japanese party and its extensive equippage arrived in Washington on May 14th and was the source of much entertainment for the following month:

> *"The Embassy has eighty tons of baggage, a large amount of treasure, and fifteen large boxes of presents for the President of the United States; among which are several very handsome rifles, manufactured at Yedo, and are an ingenious improvement upon the Sharpe rifle. They also bring with them about eighty thousand dollars in cash, with which to make purchases in this country. This money was brought from Japan in silver, and changed in San Francisco for American gold.*
>
> *The personnel of the Embassy, servants and all, numbers seventy-one, of whom twenty are officials; one having taken ill at Aspinwall was sent home."*[11]

The Willards turned over an entire floor to the Japanese, specially refurbished for the occasion. They were given sole use of the Fourteenth Street entrance, one of the kitchens and private dining facilities. Throughout their visit, the ever curious Japanese studied the Americans who in turn found the Japanese fascinating. The visitors were entertained at several ceremonies of introduction and diplomatic exchange, but none as solemn as the presentation of the treaty to President Buchanan.

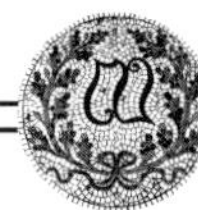

Richard & Marie Carr Collection

Japanese Greeting Ladies in Willard Lobby

Due to the significance of the occasion, the White House was filled with official and unofficial onlookers:

"The President then entered, followed by his Cabinet, and took, not indeed the positions originally intended for them, (these were irrecoverably gone,) but still a conspicuous place in front of the ladies.

After a pause, the three Japanese princes charged with the custody of the treaty entered the apartment, and, after advancing a few paces, bowed reverently; took a few more steps, and bowed again, with all the rigid formality of the toy called a "mandarin;" and, having bowed once more as they approached the President, they then stood fast. They were magnificently dressed, as above described. The caps, or ornaments, which they wore upon their heads, they retained throughout the ceremonies. The dimness of the light in the room would have led to the impression that they were middle aged men, of a complexion between sallow and Indian red, and that they were richly dressed in female apparel.

The Ambassador in chief, who stood in the center, now read from a paper which he held in his hand his speech, or official address to the President. It was read with a rather strong nasal intonation, indicating earnestness rather than

eloquence. This speech was interpreted as follows:

'His Majesty, the Ty-coon, has commanded us that we respectfully express to his Majesty the President of the United States, in his name, as follows:

Desiring to establish on a firm and lasting foundation the relations of peace and commerce so happily existing between the two countries that lately the plenipotentiaries of both countries have negotiated and concluded a treaty, he has now ordered us to exchange the ratification of the treaty in your principal city of Washington. Henceforth he hopes that the friendly relations shall be held more and more lasting, and he is very happy to have your friendly feeling: and pleased that you have brought us to the United States, and will send us to Japan in your men of war.'

When the Ambassador concluded this address, a square red sort of box or bundle was, with some delay, unfolded, and its contents presented ceremoniously and with an official air to the President, containing, as we suppose, a letter to the President from the Tycoon, or Chief Magistrate of Japan, and which the President immediately handed over to Mr. Secretary Cass, who stood on his left hand."[12]

The entire ceremony took just over one hour and was a magnificent spectacle with both sides formally attired and supported by Japanese and U.S. military escorts as well as the marine band. The reporter only complained of the heaviness of the speeches because of their labored translation first into Dutch and then into Japanese.

The embassy seems to have been well pleased with their accommodations, and they were forever curious about American dress and custom. The use of their own kitchen enabled them to survive some of the local culinary heresies, such as drowning rice in butter or sugar as well as the local's predisposition towards meat and fat. One interesting observation from a Japanese diary was written after they attended a ball at Secretary Cass' residence:

"Immediately after we were seated the music commenced, and an officer in uniform with one arm round a lady's waist and the other hand holding one of hers, started moving around the room on his toes, many others following his example. Upon inquiring we were told that this was a 'dance.'

As I watched the various movements of the dancers I could not help smiling at the way in which the very large skirts, called crinoline, which the ladies wore, increased in volume until they became of enormous proportions when the dancers attained their top speed.

This continued until midnight. As for us we had never seen or imagined anything like it before. It was of course with no small wonder that we had witnessed this extraordinary sight of men and bare-shouldered women hopping around the floor arm in arm, and our wonder at the strange performance became so great that we began to doubt whether we were not on another planet. I need not say that we did not remain until midnight."[13]

Although not infrequently mobbed and gawked at, our Japanese guests had an exciting experience. The Ambassador was very taken with the Navy Yard and its modern, steam driven machinery. The Japanese also profitted culturally in many ways from their visit. Within a month, the treaty was formally ratified, and the popular visitors departed for Japan. Life at the Willard returned to normal.

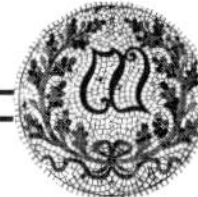

Martin Luther King Library, Washingtoniana Collection

Pennsylvania Avenue in 1861

Chapter II

COMING OF AGE

Kiplinger Washington Collection

The Willard–Late 1890's

As with any war, there is some profit as well as pain and suffering, the Civil War was no exception. Washington became a focal point of political and military activity, and its hotels were much in demand. One historian reported that hotels, including the Willard, were able to double their prices from two dollars to four dollars per night, and still the demand was unrelenting.

The Willard could not have gotten off to a more auspicious start. Already a discrete neutral ground, with Northerners entering on Pennsylvania Avenue and Southerners on F Street, it sponsored the last real effort to avert the war, the Peace Convention headed by ex-President John Tyler. It was home to Abraham Lincoln prior to his inauguration, and it was the setting for some famous lines from Julia Ward Howe, Walt Whitman and Nathaniel Hawthorne, as well as being the focal point for other important events. Being at the hub of Washington, Willard's inevitably became a center of political activity throughout the war.

Hopeless as it was, on the eve of the Civil War, there were still calm heads who would have averted the war, if at all possible. The last significant effort towards this end was the Peace Convention chaired by ex-President John Tyler and held in Willard Hall. The aspirations of many were great, but the gulf between the states was already too wide to bridge without force of arms:

> *"Washington, Monday February 4, 1861 The Commissioners from the several states who may be in the city of Washington are requested to meet at the Concert Hall of Willard's Hotel this day at 12 o'clock."*

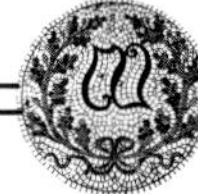

Richard & Marie Carr Collection

The Peace Convention

The Commissioners Convention:

"We need not remind our readers that this is the day fixed for the meeting in this city of the Commissioners appointed by many of the Southern and Northern States with a view to the adjustment of the unhappy controversy which already threatens our Union with total disruption. In invoking for the deliberations of this convention a spirit of wisdom and counsel and conciliation, we are sure we echo the consenting prayer of a great majority of our countrymen, who will mark the proceedings of this body with a solicitude second to that which has attached to no similar meeting in our civil history. Under such circumstances, we cannot doubt that every member will act with a deep and solemn sense of his responsibility in the sight of God and fellow-citizens throughout the whole land. And not only the present generation, but our descendants to the latest posterity may be said to have an interest for weal or woe in the complexion which each constituent of the body shall contribute by his counsels to impress on the result of its deliberations. In the presence of such animating motives to high and dignified consultation, we do not permit ourselves to suppose that the golden hours of this critical period will be wasted in frivolous debate, joined on immaterial or secondary issues, but on the contrary we cannot doubt that each member will so guard his language and his spirit that, in addressing himself to this great transaction, no word shall be dropped which (if indeed the public shall be admitted at all to the audience of the Convention) will tend to increase the feverish excitement of the times."[14]

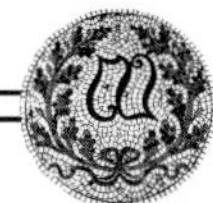

Despite these sentiments and ideals, Mr. Tyler was forced to report to Mr. Lincoln that the efforts of the convention had failed.

Lincoln's arrival in Washington was not without some excitement. With war fever building emotions, feelings in Maryland, strongly sympathetic to the Southern cause, were reaching dangerous levels, and there arose some concern for the President-Elect's safety as he passed through Baltimore en route to Washington. Because of this concern, Alan Pinkerton, the soon to be famous detective, brought Lincoln into Washington ahead of schedule, and by some accounts in disguise, where he took up lodging at Parlor No. 6 on the second floor of The Willard. This slight deception was a source of consternation to the public at large and to Mrs. Lincoln, but it was accomplished, nonetheless, without incident.

> *"General expectation and the outgivings of the newspapers for the two or three latter days of last week placed the arrival of the President-Elect in the Federal metropolis as likely to happen on the afternoon of Saturday last. The natural consequence was that thousands of our citizens of both sexes came to a ready determination to witness his personal entrance to the city if the weather would permit. But this 'well laid scheme' was frustrated by the report, which gathered wings on Saturday morning for some hours before noon, that Mr. Lincoln had already arrived in Washington and was quietly lodged at Willard's Hotel. It took some time for people to get themselves to believe the statement of this fact, but, as witnesses multiplied, incredulity herself was obliged to give in.*

Lincoln's Willard Registry

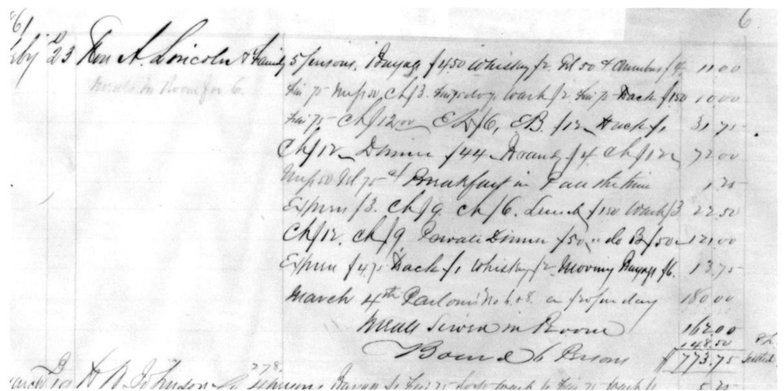

The Willard Family Papers, Library of Congress

> *Two or three reports are abroad as to the motives which induced Mr. Lincoln to anticipate the publicly announced time of his arrival in Washington. One is that he was telegraphed to be present here for reasons of State before the separation of the Peace Convention; a second that he was telegraphed by official parties here to come on in advance of the announced time in order to prevent possible disturbances that might grow out of conflicting purposes of political clubs in Baltimore— of the Republican Clubs to honor Mr. Lincoln with a public demonstration and of their far more numerous opponents to prevent it. Our own solution is that, under all the circumstances of the case, which we doubt not Mr. Lincoln himself correctly appreciated, he deemed it would be best to avoid all chances of turmoil, and at the same time to be relieved of all further demonstrations, of which his journey had been already amply full.*

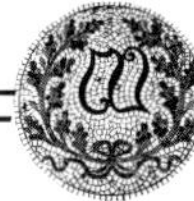

Matthew Brady

Abraham Lincoln–February 27, 1860

Mr. Lincoln was met at Willards' Hotel by Hon. Wm. H. Seward, who had been waiting there for him; a suite of rooms having been engaged at that hotel for Mr. Lincoln the day before. After breakfast, Mr. Lincoln, accompanied by Mr. Seward, called on the President of the United States, who was holding a Cabinet session at the time. After a few minutes conversation in the private reception room of the President, Mr. Lincoln was conducted to the council room and there introduced to the members of the cabinet, by all of whom he was received in a very cordial manner. After leaving the Presidential Mansion, the President-Elect and Mr. Seward paid a brief visit to General Scott, and then returned to the hotel. Fatigued by a long journey and loss of rest, Mr. Lincoln retired for a few hours' sleep, after which, in the evening, he was called upon by many Senators and Representatives, and the members of the Peace Convention in a body paid him a visit.

Mrs. Lincoln and her children, with accompanying friends, passed over the road by the usual day train from Harrisburg, and they encountered in the depot in Baltimore a crowd estimated at fifteen thousand persons, whose disappointment at finding that the President-Elect had gone forward in the morning was great and found loud and various expression. Most ample arrangements had been made in Baltimore to receive him. The full police force were at the depot, and all good citizens were anxious to show that there was no foundation for apprehended danger.

It will be unnecessary to apprise our own citizens of the fact that ample preparations had been made by our city authorities for the worthy reception of the President-Elect in the Federal City. A considerable number of carriages to convey Mr. Lincoln, family, and attendants had been engaged, and whoever else would have been appropriate to the occasion."[15]

In his haste to come to Washington, it seems that Lincoln forgot his slippers. Realizing that no foot in the hotel was large enough to require a slipper as large as Lincoln, Henry Willard hastened across the street to borrow a pair from his wife's grandfather who happened to be paying the family a visit.

The Willard Family Collection

The Slippers Lincoln Borrowed

Times were tough indeed facing the President-Elect. Southern states were rebelling, the Peace Convention had failed and the winds of war were fanned by nearly every conversation and debate. Times notwithstanding, there was still opportunity for the town to learn of the new president-to-be's sense of humor. "Lincoln's first levee was held not in the White House but at Willard's Hotel, some days before the inauguration. The higher public functionaries and their wives, had been notified rather than invited to come to the hotel on a certain evening for a first glance of the new chief magistrate. Into this presence stalked the lank, loose jointed, oddly clad 'Old Abe' with his little, simple, white-shawled wife at his elbow, and the never failing jest on his lips as he made his own announcement, 'Ladies and Gentlemen, let me present to you the long and the short of the Presidency!'"[16]

President Lincoln was sworn in and the nation girded for war, as did the hotel. "Willard is preparing for war, furling all sails for the storm. The dinner table is shorn of cartes and the tea table reduced to the severe simplicity of pound cake." Just a little over a month after the President was sworn in, news came that Fort Sumter had been taken and the nation was at war. Lincoln called for seventy five thousand militia for three months, but there was a great unease in the city and much talk of the capture of the City of Washington. During these early days of danger, the city relied on local militia and the loyalty of those people available in town. A meeting was held at Willard Hall to organize protection while waiting for reinforcements from regular army to the north. Two companies were raised, the Clay Battalion and the Frontier Guards. The Frontier Guards were stationed around the White House and Clay's Battalion was stationed at Willard Hall with the responsibility of patrolling the streets at night.

During these early months, the Willard was involved in another incident which made the cover of *Harper's Weekly.* A fire broke out in a neighboring building and some of the troops stationed in Washington rallied to save the hotel, led by a young Colonel who had been clerk to Lincoln.

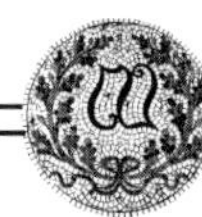

"Colonel Ellsworth detailed ten men from each company, and led them on a run down the avenue. They broke down the door of the Franklin engine house, and dashed across the street, followed by most of the remaining members of the regiment, who had knocked down the sentries at the doors and leapt from the windows of the Capitol at the cry of fire. A large crowd on the Avenue, including the guests of the hotel in varied wardrobes, watched the Zouaves expertly mounting lightening rods, and climbing into windows. They formed themselves into human ladders for passing up water buckets, and one man was suspended head first from the burning roof to reach the hose line. Suddenly, a Union flag on the roof quivered and fell. Secessionists in the crowd made mocking comments, but some Zouaves caught the flag and waived it, and Willard's hastily ran up two flags in a roar of cheers. With an exhibition fire drill and a patriotic demonstration, a calamity had been averted. The tailor shop was in ruins, but Willard's was saved.

By breakfast time, in spite of a smell of smoke and some water damage, the hotel was doing business as usual. Servants cleaned the floors and washed the windows, while in the dining room, the Zouave heroes breakfasted with the guests, on Mr. Joseph Willard's invitation."[17]

Unfortunately, Colonel Ellsworth soon thereafter became one of the early casualties of the war. While Washington was bracing for a possible attack, a confederate flag was spied flying from the Marshall House, a tavern in Alexandria. Ellsworth stormed up to the roof of the tavern and tore the flag down. As he was coming back down the stairs, he was shot dead by the innkeeper.

HARPER'S WEEKLY.

A JOURNAL OF CIVILIZATION.

Vol. V.—No. 230.] NEW YORK, SATURDAY, MAY 25, 1861. [SINGLE COPIES SIX CENTS. $2 50 PER YEAR IN ADVANCE.

WILLARD'S HOTEL, WASHINGTON, SAVED BY THE NEW YORK FIRE ZOUAVES.—Sketched by our Special Artist.—[See Page 331.]

Richard & Marie Carr Collection

Zouaves Fighting a Fire Next to the Willard

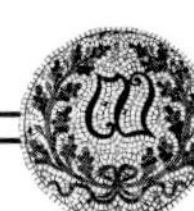

Martin Luther King Library, Washingtoniana Collection

Willard's During the Civil War

Not long after Ellsworth's death, North and South engaged in their first test of strength near Washington at Bull Run. Civilian groups, including genteel ladies, had gathered at the battle site in picnic fashion to observe the Northern troops rout the Southerners and hasten the conclusion of the war. This illusion was quickly dispelled, and the Northern soldiers, bloodied and beaten, made their way back to the City in disarray. In the aftermath, already showing his compassion for the common soldier, Walt Whitman penned these harsh lines:

"There you are, shoulder straps, but where are your companies? Where are your men? Incompetents! Never tell me of chances of battle, of getting stray'd and the like. I think this is your work, this retreat, after all. Sneak, blow, put on airs in Willard's sumptuous parlors and bar-rooms, or anywhere.

No explanation will save you. Bull Run is your work; had you been half or one-tenth worth your men, this would never have happened."[18]

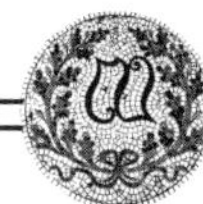

In the fall of that same year, another poem was penned that would ring across the nation for decades to come. Julia Ward Howe had traveled to Washington with some of the early promoters of the Sanitary Commission. While returning to the City from an excursion, her carriage had become surrounded by marching regiments and she and her companions sang songs to pass the time, one of which was "John Brown's Body lies a-molding in the grave." One of her traveling companions, not caring for those words, remarked that Mrs. Howe should write her own words for that tune. The next morning, lying awake in the gray early light before dawn in her room at the Willard, Mrs. Howe had the immortal words of the Battle Hymn of the Republic come to her as if in a dream. Before the coming of dawn, she arose and quickly inscribed the words, as if in a poem, which she would later, when arising, decipher in near disbelief.

The poem was published in the *Atlantic Monthly* for February, 1862 and so gripping were the words, that they became almost overnight the Battle Hymn of the North. One story relating the effect of these words concerns a Chaplain McCabe.

> *"When some time after (Gettysburg), McCabe was released from prison, he told in Washington, before a great audience of loyal people, the story of his war time experiences; and when he came to that night in Libby Prison, he sang the 'Battle Hymn' once more. The effect was magical: people shouted, wept, and sang, all together; and when the song was ended, above the tumult of applause was heard the voice of Abraham Lincoln, exclaiming, while the tears rolled down his cheeks, 'Sing it again!'"* [19]

War time was a time for words from another famous American. Writing for the *Atlantic Monthly* in 1862, we find Nathaniel Hawthorne giving us a glimpse of the Willard as he covered the war.

> *". . . if compelled to pass a rainy day in the hall and parlors of Willard's Hotel, it proved about as profitably spent as if we had floundered through miles of Virginia mud, in quest of interesting matter. This hotel, in fact, may be much more justly called the centre of Washington and the Union than either the Capitol, the White House, or the State Department. Everybody may be seen there. It is the meeting-place of the true representatives of the country,—not such as are chosen blindly and amiss by electors who take a folded ballot from the hand of a local politician, and thrust it into the ballot-box unread, but men who gravitate or are attracted hither by real business, or a native impulse to breathe the intensest atmosphere of the nation's life, or a genuine anxiety to see how this life-and-death struggle is going to deal with us."* [20]

With the advent of the war, the Willard brothers, Henry and Joseph, decided to retire from the active hotel business, each taking a different direction. Henry moved to Hudson, New York where he and his family lived until 1868, when they moved back to Washington. Joseph joined the Union Army and was commissioned a Captain, later promoted to Major, on the staff of General McDowell and was involved in activities in Northern Virginia. On occasion, Major Willard was quartered at a house in Fairfax where he met and fell in love with the beautiful Antonia Ford.

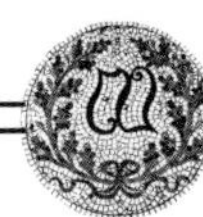

The Willard Family Papers, Library of Congress

Joseph C. Willard

As it turned out, Antonia was a confederate spy who had received a commission from General J.E.B. Stuart in 1861.

> *"To All Whom It May Concern*
> *Know Ye*
> *That reposing special confidence in the patriotism, fidelity and ability of Antonia J. Ford, I, James E.B. Stuart, by virtue of the power vested in me as brigadier general in the Provisional Army of the Confederate States of America, do hereby appoint and commission her my honorary aide-de-camp, to rank as such from this date.*
> *She will be obeyed, respected and admired by all true lovers of a [illegible word] nature.*
> *Given under my hand and seal at the headquarters of the Cavalry Brigade at Camp Beverly the 7th October, A.D. 1861, and the first year of our independence.*
> *J.E.B. Stuart"*[21]

During her involvement in the War, Antonia is credited with providing information on troop movements in Northern Virginia, and she is linked to the raid by Colonel John Singleton Mosby resulting in the capture of General Stoughton. Times caught up with Antonia and she was arrested on March 17, 1863 and taken to the Old Capital Prison. Since Antonia was a commissioned officer, Major Willard used his rank to have the right to escort her personally to prison. On this fateful journey, Willard swore that he would work to secure the freedom of Antonia Ford and her father, which he accomplished seven months later when, in September of 1863, Antonia was released after swearing an oath of allegiance to the United States.

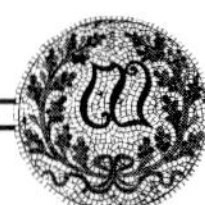

Richard & Marie Carr Collection

Early Willard Lobby

Columbia Historical Society, Washington, D.C.

The Willard in the 1870's

Willard's was known three-quarters of a century ago, as the 'City' Hotel, subsequently it was called 'Williamson's,' and later on it took the name of 'Fullers,' which it kept till some few years before the War of the Rebellion, when passing into the hands of the Willard Brothers, it was given its present name.

And how familiar the name has become throughout all the length and breadth of the land! There is not a city, scarcely a hamlet in the land where it will not awaken in many breasts pleasant and sometimes thrilling recollections. Of the vast armies which ebbed and flowed through Washington during the late war, there are thousands of old soldiers who will recall with delight the hours spent within the hospitable doors of Willard's. The old statesmen who served their country in the halls of Congress or the Cabinets of the Presidents will recall at the sound of the name, the grave and patriotic consultations which had for their object the happiness of millions of people—the welfare of the great Republic. And their successors remark upon the coincidence, that as it then was the favorite haunt, the

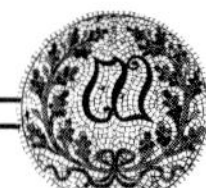

chosen council-house of those whose hands held the destinies of the Republic, so it remains and probably always will be. At the mention of the name the stately, white-haired dame, the matron of middle age, the bride of yesterday, and the newly-launched debutante alike recall the spacious parlors and drawing rooms which have been the scene of their triumphs.

From a time where of the memory of even the oldest inhabitant of the city runneth not to the contrary, our Presidents have gone from the suites of rooms on the second floor at the corner of Pennsylvania Avenue and Fourteenth Street, escorted with all the pomp and pageantry which have grown up around the ceremony, to the east front of the noble capitol building to assume the oath of their high office in the presence of waiting thousands, and to deliver their inaugural addresses which marked out the policy to be pursued by the new administration. And at other times, 'the President's Suite,' as it is properly called, has witnessed many sharp contests that have been waged over the Speakership of the House; or the sedate, select caucuses at which the leaders for the Senate decided upon the man who should be elected Vice President of the United States, pro tempore.

So that to visit Willard's has come to be one of the objects of a trip to Washington, not only to those who have been here before, but to the children and children's children of those who have lived under its home-like roof. To sit at the table where the great men of our country have sat; to live in the apartments where battles have been planned and political parties have been born or doomed to death; to attend receptions where the proud beauties of a century have held their court; to become familiar with surroundings amid which Presidents have drawn their most important state papers, and have chosen their Cabinet ministers; to meet and mingle with the the throng of distinguished men and women who still frequent Willard's; to come in contact with and study the travelers and scientists of all nations who gravitate to this central point in the American capital as naturally and invariably as the needle seeks the pole—these are the reasons why every year brings an increasing number of sojourners to Willard's. And they find a never-ending charm and pleasure in breathing the historic atmosphere, so pregnant with the memories of the great events that have marked our national progress.

And with all its marvelous prosperity, Willard's has grown and expanded to meet each new requirement till the men of the early day, who remember it so pleasantly, would utterly fail to recognize it today. The humble hostelry has developed into a building with a frontage of 150 feet at its south end on Pennsylvania Avenue, about the same at its north end on "F" street, while on Fourteenth Street it extends the entire length of the block, 350 feet. Its thick, solid walls are of brick trimmed with gray stone, and the entire exterior has just been painted a pure white, the cornices and window frames and sills picked out with subdued shades of drab and red. This has added to its beauty and gives a new idea of the magnitude of the structure.

Within, it at once impresses the visitor as an abode of refinement where the comforts and luxuries of life are dispensed to all with unostentatious but unfailing hospitality.

The main entrance, on Pennsylvania Avenue leads through a spacious corridor to the court or rotunda in which the business office is found, and where every evening the leading men of all parties and the notabilities of the nation may be found. They gather here to discuss the news of the day, spend an hour or so in pleasant intercourse with each other, or to silently glide up the wide stairway to apartments where wires are laid and plans of party management are discussed. The caucus may be held in either the Senate Chamber or the hall of the House of Representatives when the work to be done by that caucus has already been cut

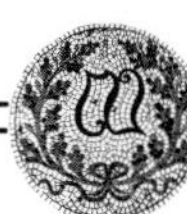

The Willard in the 1870's

out and definitely agreed upon at the consultation at Willard's. To 'meet at Willard's' at night is as much the regular thing as to perform any of the official functions of the office during the day. Here the select few outline what is to be done; at the caucus the many ratify the plan thus agreed upon.

The Court or rotunda is a magnificent room, with tessalated pavements, vaulted ceilings elaborately frescoed and supported by airy pillars with elaborately carved capitals and adorned by the skillful brush of the artist. Chandeliers and lamps in brackets, costly and elegant, fill the space with a soft and golden light, while around the walls are placed sofas upholstered in Russia leather with massive French walnut woodwork. To the right of the office as you enter is the billiard room, finished in natural woods and supplied with tables of the latest and most expensive styles; to the left is the bar, gorgeously fitted up with walnut furniture, massive mirrors and brilliant chandeliers, and stocked with the rarest wines and liquors that the vaults of Park & Tilford, the great New York house, can furnish. No expense has been spared to make the bar a model for its kind, and the employees are artists in their important profession.

To the right of the main corridor as you enter, and before you reach the rotunda is the book, news and cigar stand, controlled by Messrs. Cochran & Co., where the most fastidious smoker will find that the world has been put under contribution to gratify his taste. The whole stock of cigars, except the imported goods, are from the well-known house of Straitton & Storms, New York, whose names are a sufficient guarantee that the goods are the best the market affords. In the corridor to the left may be found the desk of Messrs. Leadingham & Co., where any style of carriage can be summoned at a moment's notice by means of the telephones which connect with their superb stables a few blocks off.

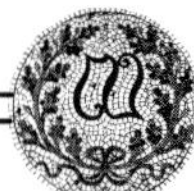

Columbia Historical Society, Washington, D.C.

The Willard in the 1880's

Columbia Historical Society, Washington, D.C.

Opposite the newsstand will be found C.A. Stewart, world-renowned and Washington's most fashionable barber, who will attend to ladies' hair in their rooms or at their residences.

The ladies' entrance, on Fourteenth Street, leads directly to the stairway, and the ground drawing room which opens into the dining room and from which communication is had with the elevator. This drawing room has few peers in the United States. It is 100 feet in length by 32 in width, and is furnished and carpeted most elaborately and luxuriously. There is scarcely an hour in the day or evening when it is not filled with groups of men and women, chatting socially as they pass to or from the dining room. This is especially the case in the evening after the late dinner, when the electric lamps lighting up the beautiful costumes of the opera and theatre parties illuminate a picture of 'fair women and brave men' never to be forgotten.

The dining room itself, stretching northward 150 feet, and filled with innumerable tables gleaming with silver and costly china, with snowy linen and neatly-dressed waiters moving swiftly and silently about, is a most agreeable and pleasing spectacle where refined people enjoy the pleasure of an unequaled table.

Upstairs, a suite of parlors, where the foot sinks into the soft carpets and gives no sound, while the light falls softly upon satin and velvet upholstery, run almost the entire length of the front on Pennsylvania Avenue, occupying in point of fact a space of 2,235 feet. Here the lady guests of the house receive callers at all times, and during nearly every day of the week hold stately and formal receptions, to which the devotees of society and fashion throng in brilliant crowds. On this same floor, opposite the parlors, is a large room—the ladies' tea room—and also used for a late breakfast room and for the large private dinner parties which

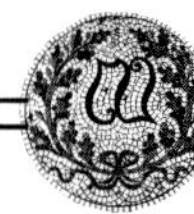

are so often given in compliment to the famous men all over the world who visit the National capital. This room is also most elaborately fitted up, and its walls and ceilings are covered with delicate frescoes which add to its charm with even the most fastidious aesthetes.

Indeed, throughout all the house, from the cellar to the attic, the rooms are furnished with all the luxuries and comforts that wealth can supply even in the costliest private residences. There are but few hotels in the world so completely and expensively furnished as Willard's.

The sanitary arrangements are as nearly perfect as man can make them. A large expense has been incurred by the present proprietor during the past summer in adapting the heating, ventilating and plumbing system to the requirements of the most recent dicta of science, and he feels warranted in assuring his guests that they need fear nothing from poisonous sewer gas or the much-dreaded malaria. His arrangements guarantee an abundance of fresh, pure air and water, and a skilled supervision will insure that perfect, equable heat at all times, which is so conducive to sound health. In respect of the health of its guests, Willard's has always borne an enviable reputation, and malaria illness has never been known in the house. The management now believe that there is a yet greater safety than there ever was before.

In this connection, the cuisine is an important matter, and it is but just to say that the cooks engaged at Willard's are not surpassed in the country. To secure them money has been but a secondary object to the proprietor, who conceives that nothing on his part should be permitted to hinder the approximate approach to perfection at which he has aimed. Whatever may have been the reputation of the table at Willard's during the past, and it has been deservedly high, the present manager is determined that it shall be exceeded.

The markets of the world contribute to the recruiting of the larder at Willard's. The delicacies of Europe, from the pâtés of Strasbourg, the sausages of Frankfort and the truffles of France, to the marmalades of Dublin, and the pickles and jellies and ginger of London, are imported expressly for the house. In the middle of winter the first shad are brought from Florida, with new potatoes, cucumbers and onions from Bermuda. Later on, the Potomac furnishes the fish-shad incomparable for flavor and richness, sheepshead and rockfish (or striped bass), and the rudely-named but delicate and delicious 'hog-fish' from Norfolk, while from the York and the Elizabeth rivers come the early vegetables of North Carolina. Oysters, not only the aristocratic Blue Points and the aldermanic Saddle Rocks from New York, but those found in the Chesapeake and its tributaries, fatter and richer and of finer flavor than any found elsewhere, are abundant for nine months in the year for the fastidious, and all the year round for those who are neither superstitious nor squeamish. From the Potomac, too, come the hard and soft-shell crabs, and the canvas-back duck with a delicacy of flavor which only the vast beds of wild celery in the waters of this region can furnish. This, without enumerating the redhead, the teal or the mallard, which almost vie with, but never quite reach, the excellence of the lordly canvas-back. That great reservior of food, Chesapeake Bay, sends its diamond-back terrapins, while Maryland furnishes the cooks who alone know the secret of serving this dainty, which gourmets cross seas to taste. From North Carolina first come the sweet and spicy cantaloupes and the huge watermelons—great, cool, green spheres filled with solidified ambrosia, crisp and melting in the mouth. Then Virginia and Maryland enter into the competition; with peaches from Delaware and grapes from the 'Eastern Shore' fit for comparison with those of the islands of Lake Erie. The vast Pastures of Mon-

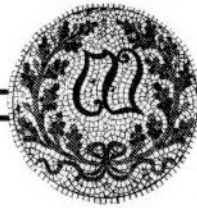

Probably by Levin Handy

The Willard for McKinley's Inauguration

The Willard in the 1890's

> *tana send the finest beef in the world; the boundless wheat fields of Dakota send via the Minnesota mills the flour that stands unrivaled; the mountains of Virginia and West Virginia and the bluegrass fields of Kentucky supply mutton, delicate and of incomparable flavor, as well as venison and wild turkeys, while game of every kind, in its season, from the prairie chicken of the West, and the pheasant of the mountains of Pennsylvania, down to the quail which pipes in the Virginia stubble, and the reed and rail birds and ortolan which feed in the vast rice fields of the Southern coast, butter balls to the eye and lusciously delicate to the palate, come at the summons of the alert purveyor intent upon the delectation of every taste. Capons from Philadelphia; golden butter from the glades of Maryland, sweet as honey and redolent with the buckwheat from clover blossoms; hams from Cincinnati; perfume of the Ohio; maple syrup from Vermont; salmon from the Penobscot and the cold, rushing streams of Canada; trout from the mountain brooks of West Virginia and Pennsylvania—where shall we find the end of that which is endless?"*[23]

During these years, the hotel still played host to notable events. In 1867, an ad appeared in a local publication for Washington's first soda fountain in Milburn's Drugstore, located in the Willard, and its "refreshing draught." In 1873, Henry M. Stanley could be found in Willard's bar recounting his adventures in Africa when, as a correspondent for the *New York Times Herald,* he tracked down Dr. David Livingston, finally locating him with the famous line, "Dr. Livingston I presume." Stanley had found Livingston, sick and out of supplies, at Ujiji near Lake Tanganyika. With Stanley's provisions, they explored the north end of Lake Tanganyika together for four months providing rich material for a book which Stanley later tried to promote in a lecture series on the advice of Mark Twain. Unfortunately, Stanley's lectures were not successful, and his book must have been somewhat suspect as it was described by Florence Nightengale as "The worst possible book on the best possible subject."

Another glamor event took place on March 1, 1883 when Leadville, Colorado silver magnate Horace Tabor married "Baby Doe" in one of the private rooms of the hotel. The newlyweds were rebuffed by the female society because they had both been divorced, but there were many prominent male dignitaries in attendance including President Chester Arthur. It was reported that one of the guests gave the bride a $75,000 diamond necklace as a wedding gift.

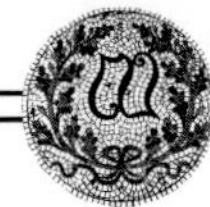

Columbia Historical Society, Washington, D.C.

The Willard–Cleveland's Inauguration, 1893

In 1897, Willard's Hall offered the first showing in Washington of a moving picture.

> *"It seems somewhat singular that Washington will have its first opportunity to see the Cinematographie Lumiere today. For the past six months, it has been the reigning novelty in New York, Boston, Philadelphia and Chicago. As a public entertainment it is still packing the theatres, and as a private entertainment it is usurping the functions of the prima donna, the tenor and the elocutionist. It is not a novelty of an hour, but has come to stay. It brings all the world with it, and shows persons and things exactly the same as they are in nature. It leaves absolutely nothing to the imagination, save sound and color. All the form, no matter how small, and all the action, no matter how swift, are reproduced with the unvarying exactness of the camera.*
>
> *Today's programme at 2 p.m., 4 p.m. and 6 p.m. at Willard Hall, will show manouvers by the soldiers of Spain, Germany and France, Royal wedding processions, street scenes, which include three here in Washington at different points along Pennsylvania Avenue, and the Puerto del Sol, Madrid, and a score of other interesting views, in all of which there is perfect action."*[24]

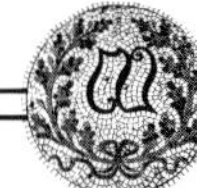

Willard Hotel Circa 1901

Columbia Historical Society, Washington, D.C.

Chapter III

THE NEW WILLARD

The advent of the 20th Century signaled a rebirth for the Willard. Joseph E. Willard was a talented entrepreneur. Raised in Fairfax and graduating from VMI, after marrying Belle L. Wyatt, he commenced what was to become an illustrious public career. Beginning in 1894, he served as a member of the Virginia House of Delegates for eight years; in the Spanish American War he served under General Fitzhugh Lee; he was Lieutenant Governor, then State Corporation Commissioner of Virginia from 1902 to 1910; and served as United States Ambassador to Spain from 1913 to 1921. While in Spain, his daughter Belle married Kermit Roosevelt who she had met through a family friendship with Theodore Roosevelt's daughter and while visiting the Roosevelt family on holiday trips.

Captain Willard, as he was known, was familiar with the Willard Hotel, aware of its history and the fact that the old patchwork structure had outlived its useful life. When he acquired the hotel, he immediately made plans for its redevelopment. Believing in the Willard's location and its natural chances for success, his plans for the hotel were grandiose. Accordingly, he engaged Henry Janeway Hardenbergh, the architect of the Waldorf-Astoria, to design a new, grand hotel on Pennsylvania Avenue. To use the words of the *Architectural Record,* "The new buildings, [Willard, Rennert & Belvedere] on the contrary, are all of them 'sky scrapers' constructed in the most grand manner and decorated with every intention of obtaining a good looking, as well as a showy, effect."[26]

Francis Benjamin Johnston, Library of Congress, Prints and Photographs Division

The Willard in 1901

Actually, the first project that Capt. Willard undertook on the block was the replacement of the old Willard Hall with a new building for the Union Trust and Storage Company. This was begun in mid-1900, then in August, the old building at the corner of Fourteenth Street and Pennsylvania Avenue was torn down to make way for the New Willard, an architectural triumph for Washington. One of the newest "sky scrapers" in the City, after the Cairo Apartments and the Post Office, The Willard was designed in the classic Beaux-Arts style with a heavy French influence. It stood one hundred sixty feet tall, on a granite base with stately columns, it had a light brick mid-section, and a stately mansard roof housing a grand ballroom with a thirty foot eliptical ceiling. As recounted in the newspapers at the time, the building was received warmly by an admiring public.

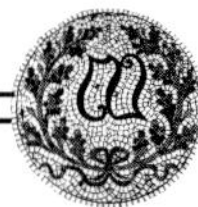

Francis Benjamin Johnston, Library of Congress, Prints and Photographs Division.

Front Desk

"The New Willard Hotel, corner of Fourteenth Street and Pennsylvania Avenue, was informally opened to the public last evening. There was no banquet, no speeches, no ceremony. The doors were simply unlocked and the register opened and placed upon the desk, ready for the signatures of patrons. The first name entered was "Thomas M. Gale," the treasurer of the new Willard Hotel Company. About fifty other signatures were added during the evening.

Although there was no dedication, the announcement that the house would open last evening called forth many hundreds of men and women, anxious to view the magnificent interior which in some respects, excels in beauty the interior of the Waldorf-Astoria, in New York City. The visitors were given the freedom of the main floor. The upper portions of the house were not open to inspection, as they are not yet fully furnished. The men's restaurant and the kitchen, both of which are in the basement, are not quite finished, although the former was open for business last night.

Probably the most gorgeous part of the hotel is the main lobby, in the southeast corner of the building, on the main floor. The entrance is from Pennsylvania Avenue. The prevailing color is of an ivory tint. Heavy red rugs are spread upon the mosaic floor and the English oak chairs and settees are upholstered in red leather. The huge marble columns and the wall and ceiling finishings give the ivory tone.

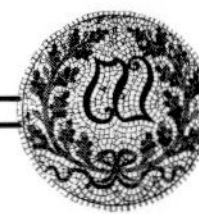

Francis Benjamin Johnston, Library of Congress, Prints and Photographs Division

Crystal Room

A corridor to the right of the entrance leads to the ladies' reception room which is one of the most beautiful spots in the house. It is a circular room, finished in pink, the furniture being of the Louis XVI design. From here is a corridor to the main restaurant, which occupies 85 feet of length of the building on Fourteenth Street.

An attractive feature of the hotel is the corridor leading from the lobby to the restaurants. This runs 90 feet, almost to the rear of the building from about the center of the north side of the lobby. On the right is the main restaurant which is 85 x 40 feet. The colors of this room are green and brown. The immense columns are mottled green marble, and the furniture and wood work is oak. The green and brown idea is carried out in the carpet and the upholstry of the chairs.

Directly across the corridor from the main restaurant is what is called the Pompeiian room. It is the restaurant for men and women where smoking is permitted. Between the main restaurant and the lobby is a balcony, upon which, the orchestra is located. Music will be furnished each evening during dinner and after the theater. At the right of the lobby, on a level with the balcony, is the east mezzanine room, which overlooks the lobby. Directly opposite are the offices of the hotel management.

Three features of the hotel are particularly noticeable throughout. These are the chandaliers, the portieres, and the rugs and carpets. The chandaliers were manufactured especially for the New Willard. An effort was made to show what magnificent work could be accomplished in this line, and the effort was a success. The chandaliers are made of a composition of bronze and brass. The portieres, rugs and carpets are of the most beautiful and richest material to be had.

The manager of the New Willard is Mr. F.S. Hight, formerly of the Waldorf-Astoria." [27]

Francis Benjamin Johnston, Library of Congress, Prints and Photographs Division

Coffee Shop

Not one to close the entire hotel operation down, Capt. Willard had the new building designed to be phased. The first phase, half-way up Fourteenth Street, was completed in 1901 while the 1858 addition to the original hotel was kept in operation. Next, the balance of the site, excluding the new Union Trust Building, was rebuilt and completed in 1904. Finally, responding to increasing business, the Union Trust Building was torn down and an addition of 61 rooms was completed in 1925. Thus was achieved a 450 room hotel with a grand design, located in the heart of the City, and with some of the finest public spaces then to be found in the nation.

The New Willard at once leapt back into the forefront of Washington hotelkeeping, and reinstated its popularity as a social center for local and national figures.

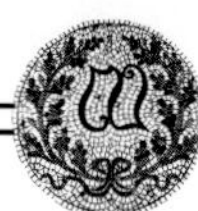

Francis Benjamin Johnston, Library of Congress, Prints and Photographs Division

Palm Court

Mark Twain was a visitor to the hotel, early recognizing the theatrical potential of the grand space presented in Peacock Alley. As reported by his biographer Albert Paine, the first time Twain went downstairs to have dinner in the New Willard, he descended by the elevator and started towards the restaurant when he realized that there was a more conspicuous way to make an entrance. With this thought, he ascended back up the elevator to a corridor where he could walk to the F Street end of the hotel and descend the regal stair with the maximum effect of his white tie attire. The effect was instantaneous.

> *"Of course he was seized upon at once by a lot of feminine admirers, and the passage along the corridor was a perpetual gantlet. I realize now that this gave the dramatic finish to his day, and furnished him with proper appetite for his dinner . . . I aided and abetted him every evening in making that spectacular descent of the royal stairway, and in running that fair and frivolous gantlet the length of Peacock Alley."*[28]

Martin Luther King Library, Washingtoniana Collection

Peacock Alley

It was there in the Red Room on February 22, 1904, that the University Club of Washington was founded. From 1905 to 1941, the hotel was home to the Gridiron Club, making a room available for their meetings on the west side of the F Street entrance. The Gridiron Club is a social club for newspapermen, with a limited membership, who gather together for an evening of merriment, speakers, and "roasting" of guests. The President is always an invited guest and frequently a target of pointed barbs. The Club rule in asserting a standard of decorum and discretion is "Ladies are always present; reporters are never present."

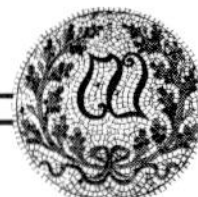

Francis Benjamin Johnston, Library of Congress, Prints and Photographs Division

Main Lobby

CONCIERGE

The Willard Family Papers, Library of Congress

President Coolidge at the Willard

women rose spontaneously to their feet and gave vent to a burst of applause that seldom had been heard in Washington."[30] Amundsen was presented with a special gold medal from the Society. At the meeting there was also the presentation of a certificate for the French Antarctic explorer Charcot and the announcement of the discovery of an old Inca City in Peru, by the Yale-National Geographic Society expedition. Of less momentus import, the dinner marked the introduction into the United States of the Chinese jujube.

1913 marked the founding of yet another club when on April 9, in the Willard dinning room, the Alfalfa Club was organized. James Calvin Hemphill, Charles Porterfield Light, Logan Waller Page and Major Robert Waterman Hunter started the tradition of an annual gathering of influential figures for a friendly evening of entertainment and comaraderie. One such evening was marked by extra curricular activity. In 1942, when President Franklin Roosevelt was attending, Washington Post publisher, Eugene Meyer, was accosted by Secretary of Commerce, Jesse Jones, who was distressed by an unfavorable editorial. Happily, the two combatants were separated before fisticufs, as it turned out that Mr. Meyer had previously taken boxing lessons from James J. Corbett in San Francisco. Interviewed the following day, the President indicated his relief at not having been called to referee. The initial group of Alfalfas grew and eventually took their lunch trade next door to the Occidental Hotel where they were afforded a private room by Gus Bucholz, formerly the headwaiter at the Willard.

In 1922, after one of the Gridiron dinners, a terrible fire destroyed the ballroom. Among the guests who were roused from their sleep were Vice President and Mrs. Calvin Coolidge, John Philip Sousa, Adolph Zukor and dozens of delegates to a D.A.R. Convention. Coolidge lived at the Willard during the entire term of his Vice Presidency, and when President Harding died, Coolidge remained at the Willard for a short time while Mrs. Harding moved out of The White House. While Coolidge was Vice President, he caught a cat-burglar in his room, but he let him go after the burglar promised to convert to the straight and narrow.

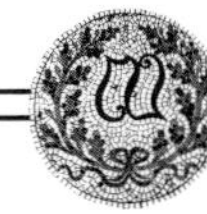

Columbia Historical Society, Washington, D.C.

Pennsylvania Avenue and the Willard Circa 1927

In the early years after 1900, the Willard Hotel had been owned by Joseph Willard, but he once again assigned its operation to others. Initially, the hotel was entrusted to Stellwagen, Gales and Hamilton. In 1921, The Capitol Hotel Company, owned by Lucius M. Boomer, a well-known hotelier assumed control. When the new hotel opened in 1901, its manager, Frank S. Hight, was lured from New York City where he had been Assistant Manager of the Waldorf-Astoria for the preceding five years. It was perhaps Hight who was responsible for the famed Peacock Alley at the Willard. That name had originated as a description of the corridor between the Waldorf's Palm Room and the Empire Room where the reigning social elite, such as the Vanderbilts and the Goulds dined. Hight ran a successful hotel under the guidance of Stellwagen, Gales and Hamilton and Boomer, including the establishment for the first time of an effective accounting system, developed by Mr. Horwath for Lucius Boomer.

In 1929, Boomer withdrew from the operation of the hotel and the Willard family, Joseph Willard's descendants, resumed control for the first time in sixty-eight years. A lease was signed, for twelve years, between The Willard Incorporated and the Virginia Hotel Company, the family entity which owned the property. The Willard Incorporated's directors included Frank S. Hight, President, John B. Swen, Secretary Treasurer, Kermit Roosevelt, Joseph W. Wyatt and Belle L.W. Willard (Joseph's wife, Joseph E. Willard had died in 1924).

Immediately, the new corporation had to cope with an economic depression and growing competition with other hotels and apartment houses. As evidenced by the records of the meetings of the corporation, costs were cut where possible; advertising was resorted to; but standards of excellence were maintained, and the Willard survived a difficult period. As an illustration, orchestra music was discontinued as of July of 1930 at a savings of $2,000 per month. Twenty-five senators and congressmen and their wives complained to the management, which prompted Hight to negotiate a new contract with the orchestra leader, Meyer Davis, to provide a four-piece orchestra to play from 7–9:00 p.m., seven nights per week for $190 per week.

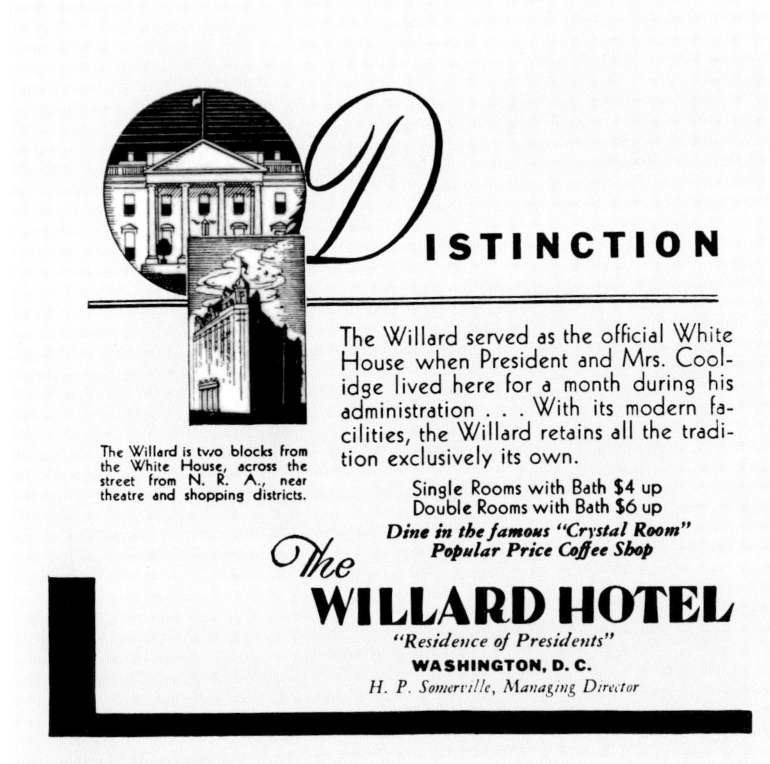

Early Advertisement

The Willard Family Papers, Library of Congress

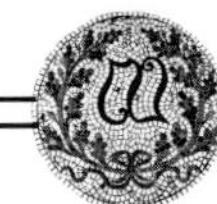

Board Meeting, November 6, 1930

"The Chairman said what everybody is interested in is economy in operation without loosing friends . . . making every savings possible without making the hotel unattractive to the public.

Mr. Conner stated that service and other expenses must be in line with the type of business of the hotel, that otherwise the volume of business would be of no value. Mr. Conner said occupancy was up and revenues down because of selling rooms and food for less money. The Chairman said the hotel is attracting a high type of patron, but many men who formerly would pay $8.00 or $10.00 for rooms and buy expensive meals, frequently now took $4.00 rooms and inexpensive meals. The Chairman thought this was a temporary condition, which was affecting all business; that by endeavoring to keep the present patrons by taking excellent care of them, and attracting new patrons of the same type, rates could be increased when business got better without driving them away.

Mr. Conner remarked that he did not approve of rate reductions or wage reductions, that every time a rate reduction in rooms or food is put into effect the public, without any real cause, says 'oh, they are slipping.'

The Chairman said that might be true in normal times but we are now in a business war. Mr. Conner did observe that rate reductions at this time did meet a popular demand. He said one reason the occupancy was up was that some former guests who went to the Mayflower had come back, and in addition the hotel got some people from the Raleigh and other houses of that type who would prefer to come to the Willard on account of the environment if they could pay about the same price. Mr. Conner stated that the 60% occupancy of rooms in the in the hotel for the month of January, was very good as compared with other hotels. Mr. Conner said the whole question centered around the length of the business life of the Willard, that Washington is going to have another high class hotel when people think the Mayflower is making money.

The Chairman stated that one new high class hotel, the Shoreham, just built, had gone into the hands of receivers. Mr. Hight said the Shoreham had affected the apartment business of the Mayflower. Mr. Conner said a new house will attract at least 40% of its trade from other hotels in the same city. The Chairman said money people went up town for awhile, but the Willard with its redecorated rooms and other improvements was getting some of them back, and would get more after Pennsylvania Avenue improvements were completed.

The Chairman said four solicitors had been employed and had produced business especially Mr. Howard, who solicited all officers of corporations, etc. in Washington which had officers and representatives visiting Washington; that the Willard is a downtown hotel and must cater especially to business men, and cannot expect to get many ladies, who only come downtown to shop and for the theatre. He said Babson's view was that the producers of this country would have to retail their goods for less money so that business could keep going. When business got better, prices could be restored. The Willard, in order to survive now, has had to cut its rates and cater to clients whose incomes have been reduced.

Mr. Conner said days of normal rates were many years away, about seven or eight . . . "[31]

Francis Benjamin Johnston, Library of Congress, Prints and Photographs Division

Ladies' Entrance

Board Meeting January 23, 1931

"The Chairman reported that Mr. Hight had reduced the rates for table d'hote meals in all rooms to meet competition. Mr. Hight said he hoped the $1.00 lunch and the $1.50 dinner in the Crystal Room would attract shoppers. The Chairman said that because people went to the Washington Coffee Shop, where prices were lower, the Willard Coffe Shop was now serving a $ .75 lunch without dessert, an $ .85 lunch with simple dessert, hot and cold plates for $ .50, $ .60, $ .75 to $1.00, and maintained the regular $1.00 lunch. Mrs. Willard said people did not want a large lunch. The Chairman stated that one of the hotel's best patrons said $1.00 was more than he wanted to pay now for lunch, and the food more than he frequently wanted to eat."[32]

Board Meeting April 13, 1932

"Mr. Conner stated that the trend of business in Washington during March, 1932 was down 5%, whereas at the Willard it was up 7%, a difference of 12% . . . he pointed out that the decline in food revenue was caused by the large number of people registering in the hotel for the prestige and eating out in the dozens of cheaper eating places near the Willard. Mr. Horwath suggested that Mr. Hight have signs reading 'Clean Laundry Packs Better' (used in Hotel New Yorker) placed on closet doors in the rooms, in an effort to increase the laundry business."[33]

In October of 1932, Frank S. Hight resigned as President of The Willard Incorporated and as General Manager of the hotel after 32 years of service. Belle L.W. Willard assumed the responsibilities of President of the Corporation, and Harry P. Sommerville was appointed Managing Director in Hight's place.

Board Meeting, December 12, 1932

"Mr. Sommerville then reported on various matters. He said that the Meyer Davis orchestra of four pieces, playing for dinner, now cost $135 per week against $200 per week last year. Three girls play at noontime, violin, cello and piano, and receive in return the use of the two inside rooms and three meals per day in the Coffee Shop with no cash payment. Mr. Sommerville stated that he had joined the National Press Club as an associate member, paying the initiation fee and dues out of his own pocket. If he later finds the membership beneficial to the hotel, he will ask the hotel to reimburse him. He stated that the hotel made a contribution this year to the Community Chest of $500, the same amount given last year. In addition, he personally gave $100, and 100% of the employees gave approximately $600 as against $241 last year. The Director of the Chest expressed his pleasure at the Chest luncheon at the hotel, and said the Willard this year was 100% for the first time. The next day Mr. Sommerville booked the Chest for next year, which will mean about $5,000 in food business.

Mr. Sommerville reported that he had had an airplane sign of aluminum letters 18 feet wide by 144 feet long painted on black on the roof of the hotel, and expects to get a good deal of publicity there. Will try to get Assistant Secretary Trubee Davis on to make some statement, and will have a picture of the sign taken from the air. If thought desirable, the sign could be floodlighted at night."[34]

Board Meeting, February 12, 1933

"It was reported that 200 old brass beds were sold at $ .50 each. The beauty parlor was paying $70 per month and Mrs. Belle Willard said she would contact Elizabeth Arden upon her return to New York to see if they would be interested in opening a shop in the Willard."[35]

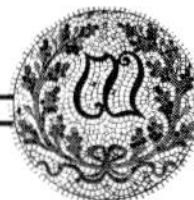

The Willard Family Papers, Library of Congress

Rooftop Advertising

As the Willard family assumed the reins of managment, even with the troubled times, the Willard remained the center of special events in Washington. In 1934, Max Baer, heavyweight boxing champion of the world, dined in the Willard Coffee Shop where he met Mary Sullivan, the manager. Two of Miss. Sullivan's favorite customers were Eleanor Roosevelt and Herbert Hoover, both of whom warned her of her involvement with Baer, a flashy dresser and intriguing personality. Despite the warnings, however, the two fell in love and were married in 1935.

The first air conditioning was installed in the hotel in 1934, and it was part of a $500,000, 1937 remodeling program which included the installation of a bath in every room. In 1940, the entire ninth floor of the hotel was leased by the British Purchasing Commission which bought aircraft and other war materials for England. Thus began the Willard's involvement with World War II. In October of 1941, the hotel opened the first experimental booth for the sale of Defense savings bonds, stamps and tax-anticipation notes. In September of 1942, Harry Sommerville resigned from the Willard as manager and was succeeded by Marshall H. Jones. Also in September, the Willard clock, a fixture on F Street since 1902, was cut down and added to the scrap-iron pile for the war effort.

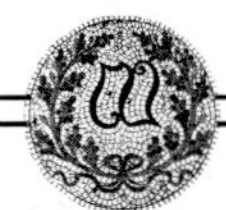

As World War II called more men to service, women became a larger segment of the Washington work force. The *Washington Post* reported in October 1942 that the Willard currently employed six girl elevator operators and was building up to a staff of nine. In December, 1942, after her performance at the National Theatre, Ruth Gordon walked the half block to the Willard and married Hollywood movie director Garson Kanin, with an assemblage that included the cast of "The Three Little Sisters" and Justice Felix Frankfurter and his wife. In August, 1942, "girl" reporter Patricia Grady reported that the Willard had installed a Miss North as "the first girl bell captain the Capital has glimpsed." Also in 1942, while the Gridiron Club was meeting in its all male splendor, the National Women's Press Club simultaneously produced its own political satire in the Willard.

The Willard business accelerated during the War. The hotel was compelled to establish a policy of not allowing guests to book more than five or six nights stay so that rooms might be available for other travelers. If there was a problem, management referred the enquiring guest to the Defense Hotel Room Clearing Bureau or the Defense Housing Bureau across Pennsylvania Avenue in the U.S. Information Building. In 1944, present day Crystal Room was opened for the first time as the Willard Room with great success and the ballroom made into a summer theater.

With the war's end, the Willard family sold the hotel. After almost one hundred years of association with the Willard family, the hotel became the property of the Abbell Hotel Company for a price of $2,800,000.

Richard & Marie Carr Collection

Willard Fashion Show

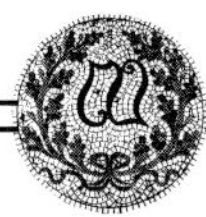

Wide World Photos

Willard Hotel–1968

Chapter IV

Last Walk Down Peacock Alley

THE END OF AN ERA

The transfer of the Willard to the Abbell Hotel Company marked the first time in a century that the hotel had not been in the Willard family's control. It also brought with it some dire predictions:

> *"Farewell, Peacock Alley . . . No more will fashionable Washington meet in the famous old promenade of the Willard; no more will blushing, happy lassies in their new raiment sway slowly a'down the length of the alley as seated matrons whisper and seated swains gape."*[36]

Reports were that Peacock Alley was to be converted to a shopping area and the ballroom to a supper club. Whether the Peacock Alley story was true or not is problematical; it was true, however, that Harry Anger and Paul Young had proposed to spend $100,000 to convert the ballroom to a night club with top entertainers. In July, 1946, the ABC Board refused to grant a liquor license for the club, thus killing the proposal. The reasons given for the rejection were inadequate fire exits and the impossibility of sealing off the club from the rest of the hotel.

As the New Willard passed its fifty year mark, it was once again showing signs of deterioration. It had been build prior to air conditioning and other modern conveniences and constant remodeling was essential. It still possessed some of the finest public spaces in the city, but much of the original beauty had faded. The ballrooms had been burnt out in 1922 and were not used for public functions since the mid-thirties.

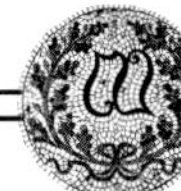

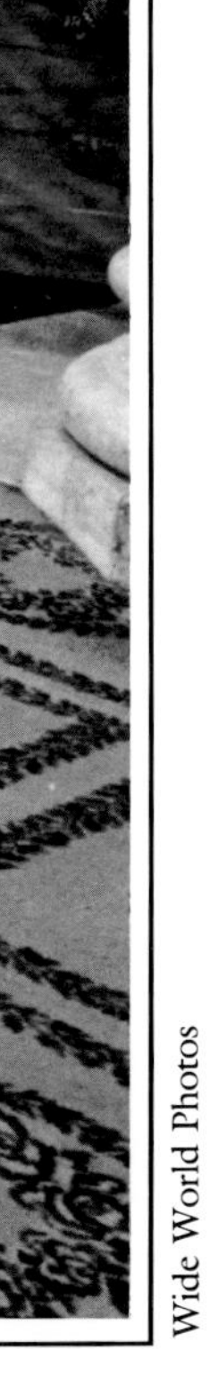

Wide World Photos

Final Check-Out–July 15, 1968

The discussions between the owners and the government were interrupted in 1968 by the decision to close down the hotel. Hotel revenues had declined steadily since 1966 to the point where the Abbell Company had been behind in its payments to the owners on more than one occasion. The situation worsened with April riots, and because of the new Pennsylvania Avenue Plan, there did not appear to be any reason to make further investments in the building. Benenson and his partners paid off the Abbell group and cancelled their lease; then they closed the hotel on July 15, 1968. Guests received a "dear guests" letter under their doors and the employees were given notice that the hotel operation had been terminated.

With the Willard's closing, Benenson was quoted as saying that the future of the hotel was up to the Temporary Commission on Pennsylvania Avenue. Chairman Owings used the occasion to comment that the closing might speed the renewal of Pennsylvania Avenue and that the hotel should be torn down to make way for the planned National Square. He also stated that the Commission would discourage any new investment in the hotel.

Closing the Willard also marked another turning point, that relating to public opinion. The Pennsylvania Avenue Plan for the Willard had been approved by the National Capital Planning Commission and the Commission on Fine Arts with only one dissenting voice, that of Elizabeth Rowe. With the hotel actually closed, however, the sentiments of years of fond memories began to trickle into the newspapers and preservationists began to organize to save the hotel as they had been fighting to save the old Post Office building just down the street.

Wide World Photos

Closing Down the Willard

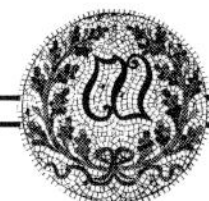

Copyright Washington Post; Reprinted by Permission of D.C. Public Library

Traveler's Aid Ball

Closed though its doors were, the Willard was host to a few activities in its waning years. The United Citizens for Nixon-Agnew leased four floors of the hotel in the fall of 1968 to work for the election of Richard M. Nixon. One of the earliest public actions to save the Willard was a letter from the Federation of Citizen Associations asking President-Elect Nixon to place the Willard and the Occidental Restaurant on the national register of historic places in order to block the plan for National Square.

On July 1, 1969, the Travelers Aid Society hosted a charity ball on the ground floor of the hotel and guests danced to strains of "Poor Butterfly" and "Look for the Silver Lining" from the orchestra of Emery Davis, whose father, Meyer Davis had gotten his start at the Willard in 1919. The last two users of the old building were a United Air Lines ticket office and Fahrney's Pens, who occupied self-contained spaces on F Street and managed to stay on until the early 1970's.

The Johnson Administration came and went, and no agreement was reached on a trade property; so the Willard owners began making plans for themselves. They had an office building designed to replace the hotel in early 1969 which was rejected by the Fine Arts Commission because it conflicted with the plan for National Square. This ruling was taken up with the City's Corporation Counsel which, in turn, ruled that the permit to build the office building should not be denied. Through Vlastimil Koubek, architect for the owner, an application was filed for a permit to tear the building down in October of 1969. Between November of 1969 and March of 1970, all of the furniture, fixtures and equipment of the hotel was sold to the public at auction. One surprise was the outpouring of

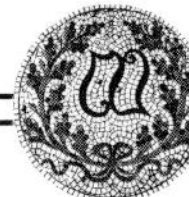

public interest at the auction. "I had expected 1,300" the auctioneer said. "I guess we had about 13,000 and 11,000 of those are mad at us because they couldn't get in." Over the course of those few months, everything in the hotel that was not nailed down was sold, along with some things that were. Demand was so great that the auctioneer raised his admission price from his original $1.00 to $7.50 in order to reduce the number of "lookers." Nostalgia had a high price and the result was that the building was thoroughly stripped.

In 1970, GSA came up with two viable potential sites that could be used in a Willard trade. One was a 17 acre site in Arlington which was once the home of the Navy Waves. Benenson had the Charles F. Smith Co. prepare a plan for the Virginia site but the swap never got beyond a conditional contract for exchange. Local citizen and political opposition forced GSA to cancel the deal. Plans to try to use Miller Field on Staten Island never got beyond local opposition either, and finally faded away in mid-1972. During the same time period, legislation was introduced to establish a federal Bicentennial Development Corporation to implement the Pennsylvania Avenue Plan, but the bills never got out of committee. Finally on October 27, 1972, Congress created the Pennsylvania Avenue Development Corporation (PADC), but it did not authorize or appropriate any funds which could be used to buy the Willard. The PADC legislation did carry with it, however, a one-year moritorium on rebuilding on the Avenue.

Exasperated by the swap exercise and the city's permit process, the owners began a game of legal cat and mouse that was to go on for five years. They filed for a permit in November, 1973 to convert the building to an office building, including

Wide World Photos

Auctioning the Willard's Contents

The Auction

stripping off the facade. On November 21, the Fine Arts Commission once again stopped the owners from going ahead with their plans. This action was deemed critical by the City as it had not yet passed its delay in demolition regulations to protect landmark buildings. On December 31, 1973, the Willard owners filed suit in D.C. Superior Court to force the City to either issue the permits they had applied for or to buy the building.

As time passed, public opinion worked its way into the offices of the planners who were revising the 1964 plan for Pennsylvania Avenue. In January, 1974, John Woodbridge, the Executive Director of PADC, was quoted as saying that the plan to remove the Willard was not the desired plan, but that because of the uncertainty around the public cost of such an undertaking, he guessed as much as $20 million, saving the hotel was doubtful. By the fall of 1974, however, PADC had come full circle, and its new plan called for preserving the hotel. Coincidentally, on October 1, 1974, Congress enacted new PADC legislation which created a new building moritorium lasting til June 30, 1975 unless the new Pennsylvania Avenue Plan became effective by that date. As it happened, the Plan became effective on May 19, 1975.

One of the key reasons PADC had reversed itself on the Willard was a report prepared by a private developer which answered the questions about the best use of the hotel and the amount of subsidy actually required to carry out a plan to put the building back in service. Early in 1974, realizing that the uncertainty over what to do with the Willard was as great a problem as funding, Lawson B. Knott, Jr., then Executive Director of the National Trust for Historic Preservation, led the National Trust in co-sponsoring with the National Park Service a study to evaluate the re-use of the hotel. The Oliver T. Carr Company conducted the study along with Vlastimil Koubek, the George Hyman Construction Company and Inter·Continental Hotels. After analyzing seven different alternatives including office, hotel, condominium and mixed use, the Carr Company concluded that hotel use was the most economically practical option for the redevelopment of the hotel, and that the amount of public subsidy required would be $5,000,000. A report was produced on October 1, 1974 which was added to the Pennsylvania Avenue Plan when it was submitted to Congress.

In June, 1974, the D.C. Superior Court ruled in favor of the Willard owners for a demolition permit, and this decision was later affirmed by the Court on December 10, 1974 which further stated that if the City continued to deny the owners their demolition permit, it would be straying into the area of inverse condemnation. No sooner had the court ruled in favor of the owners, than a new lawsuit was filed by Frank H. Rich and Don't Tear It Down, Inc. to prevent the issuance of a permit on the grounds that the PADC building moritorium was in effect and the Willard owners had not received the approvals from PADC necessary to proceed. PADC notified the Mayor on December 27th of its objections to the permit; the City notified the Court of PADC's objections on February 26,1975 and of its determination to not issue the permit; and, on August 26, 1975, the Court prevented the owners from altering the hotel facade in any way without the approval of PADC.

While all of this legal maneuvering was proceeding, there were submitted a series of ideas and proposals for saving the Willard, all of which were rejected but served to keep hope alive. In the fall of 1974, Congressman Joe Moakley from

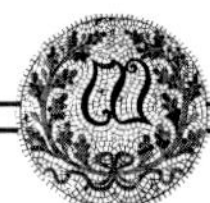

Final Days

Massachusetts introduced legislation to have the government buy the hotel and renovate it for housing for Congressional pages and interns. That same fall, the Carr Company offered to buy the hotel from the owners. In January, 1975, a group claiming to represent a National American Indian organization made an offer to buy the hotel but never made it to the settlement table. In May, 1976, there was a proposal to form a National Energy Museum Foundation supported by 60 companies each contributing $1.5 million to be used to buy the Willard and turn it into a National Energy Museum.

Dreams and plans notwithstanding, in late 1975 and 1976, events finally began to take place which would end the saga of frustration over the future of the Willard. With their last loss before the Courts, the hotel owners filed a suit for inverse condemnation which was won on January 26, 1977. On a parallel course, PADC had appropriations authorized on August 14, 1976 including funds specifically earmarked for the preservation of the Willard Hotel as a demonstration project. Finally, the tug-of-war over the future of the hotel came to a close. A settlement procedure was negotiated with the owners during the balance of the year and on January 12, 1978, the government, through the PADC, took title to the Willard. Sixteen years after plans for Pennsylvania Avenue had begun to take shape: ten years after the hotel had been closed, its future as a restored landmark on Pennsylvania Avenue was finally assured. As Senator Moynihan pointed out at the groundbreaking ceremonies several years later, the rescue of the Willard resulted in a large part from government effort, but the saving of the Willard was also due in no small measure to the willingness of Charles Benenson and his partners to work with the government when they had little to sustain them but faith and hope.

Carol M. Highsmith

Lobby in Ruins

Carol M. Highsmith

Ballroom Ruins

Chapter V

A NEW BEGINNING

The new year, 1978, brought with it an announcement that the preservationists had been anticipating for five years. The government, in the form of PADC, acquired the Willard. Unfortunately, a local newspaper article also reported that the hotel was in a state of "serious disprepair." Closed since 1968, the building had at first been minimally maintained, but its condition had deteriorated dramatically after ten years of neglect. The slate roof had worn out and was leaking; parts of the gutters had fallen off; windows were broken; and the rain and cold weather took a severe toll of the building. When PADC acquired the property, it attempted to stabilize the building and move quickly to select a developer to restore it.

Later that spring, PADC issued a prospectus calling for developers to submit proposals to restore and preserve the Willard. Now a center of attention, by the end of July, nine teams had responded to the offering on the Willard including some of the best hotel companies in the world: Canadian Pacific Hotels with the Holywell Corp.; Dunfey Hotel Corp. with Forest City Enterprises; Fairmont Hotel Company with Stuart S. Golding; Hyatt Corp. with Hyatt-Willard Associates; Inter-Continental Hotels with The Oliver T. Carr Company; Lowes Hotels with Boston Properties; Radisson Hotel Corp. with the Radnor Corp.; Rossi-Willard Associates with 3-D International; and, Trust House Forte with MAT Associates.

Carol M. Highsmith

Examining a Bulls Eye Window

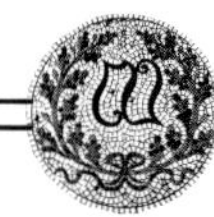

By the fall of 1978, PADC had narrowed the field from nine to three teams; Inter-Continental/Carr, Fairmont/Golding, and Trust House Forte/MAT Associates, and on December 19, 1978, the Fairmont/Golding team was selected as the new developer of the hotel. Of all of the proposals, Golding's had been the most architecturally daring. His architects, Hardy, Holzman, Pfeiffer Associates of New York, conceived a project that established an architectural anchor in the historic hotel that was repeated in an addition to be built in the center of the block and connected to the hotel at F Street. The design of the new addition was a post modern reflection of the Beaux-Art design of the original structure. Stepping down to Pennsylvania Avenue in four bays, the addition featured the same classical design elements as the original building; a solid base with formal entrance features, a subdued mid-section, and an eliptical roof, heavily ornamented with circular windows. There would be 300 rooms in the old building and 300 rooms in the new addition on top of a retail base of 65 shops, and the total project was estimated to cost $50 million.

Another feature of the winning proposal, which had been common to all entries, was that it included more than the Willard Hotel site alone. It also encompassed the land between the Washington and Willard Hotels in the middle of the block. As it happened, this property was still owned by heirs of the Willard family: the rear portion, a parking garage on F Street owned by the heirs of Henry Willard, the front portion on Pennsylvania Avenue owned by the heirs of Joseph Willard and two smaller properties, the Occidential Hotel and Restaurant being owned by the Carr Company. The Carr team had, in fact, among its members, the Joseph Willard descendants. Because of this ownership position, Carr contested the project award for several months to attempt to free up the interior site, but these efforts were to no avail.

As it turned out, the Golding team was to encounter considerable difficulty over the next three years. Golding's original team included the Fairmont Hotel Corporation and a committment to provide financing for the project at the $50 million level from the Connecticut General Life Insurance Company. Unfortunately for Golding, it turned out that he was awarded the project just before the country went into a period of high inflation, and interest rates soared from 11.5% to over 20%. During the year following the initial project award, while negotiating the ground lease for the project site and developing the plans in more detail, the total project cost increased from $50 to $75 million.

This turn of events caused Golding to begin to request what was to become several extensions of time before commencement of the project, and to change the project to increase the number of hotel rooms to over 700. Unfortunately, during a time of high inflation and increasing competition, the PADC concurrently awarded Marriott rights to build a new 700 room hotel directly across Fourteenth Street from the Willard, and the increasing size of the hotel tended to decrease the interest of lenders and investors.

In late April, 1980, the ground lease for the Willard was executed, and the developers promised to be under construction by April, 1981. Again, however, time and interest rates did not cooperate. By early 1981, the total project cost had increased to $90 million and investor interest had not improved.

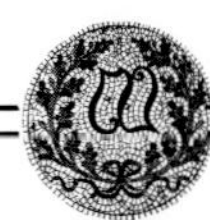

Lucian Perkins, The Washington Post

Scaffolding the Roof

Ray Lustig, The Washington Post

Under Construction

Recognizing the difficulties faced by the project, the PADC Board granted a final deadline extension to start construction to December 7, 1981. Golding worked without successful result for the better half of 1981 to line up funding for his project. Finally, with time running out, he determined that it would be in the best interest of the project to bring in a second development partner to help overcome the obstacles to progress and to increase the strength of his team. He contacted The Oliver T. Carr Company in the summer of 1981, and invited his old competitor to join with him to find a way to move the project foreward. The new team worked on the plans for the project and determined that its economic feasibility could be dramatically improved if the size of the hotel was reduced and an office component introduced into the project in place of the new hotel addition, all the while adhering to the basic project design. The effect of this change would be to reduce the risk associated with the hotel use and to increase project revenues. With this plan, the new partners were in a position to move forward.

In October, 1981, the new team of Golding and Carr went before PADC and proposed the admission of Carr to the development team and modification of the project to include 350 hotel rooms and roughly 225,000 square feet of office space over a retail component reduced by 50%. The team did propose working within the design guidelines established for the project in the original proposal. The Board, after some discussion, accepted the proposals and approved the team. The next two years were spent modifying the ground lease to provide for the revised project program, a new time table and the new members of the partnership. It was also at this point that the current group of Joseph Willard heirs was reintroduced to the partnership directing the rescue of the hotel. Their old partnership with Carr, which had controlled the land fronting on Pennsylvania Avenue next to the Willard, had been condemned, and by Carr's admission to the partnership currently controlling the Willard restoration, an avenue opened for them to rejoin the ownership of the hotel, which they happily embraced.

As the project gained momentum, two of the old team members changed. The New York architects withdrew and were replaced by the firm of Vlastimil Koubek, who had worked on the hotel since 1968. Also, the hotel operator withdrew and was replaced by Inter·Continental Hotels. At long last, in the fall of 1983, demolition of the non-essential parts of the hotel began and the project moved forward after fifteen years of uncertainty. On February 1, 1984, the new renovation work began with a ground breaking ceremony on Pennsylvania Avenue. It was announced that the hotel would open in the summer of 1986 while a large sign was unfurled on the front of the hotel stating, "The Willard is Back." With this fanfare, the time of eager anticipation began and many eyes were turned towards the hundreds of workmen who would labor over the hotel for the next two and one half years.

Physical reconstruction of the Willard had to overcome two different sets of obstacles. PADC and the National Park Service were insisting upon a true restoration of the major elements of the facade and the grand public spaces in the hotel. This work would require the use of some crafts which had not been employed in the building industry for years, and was complicated by the fact that the majority of the detailing in the public spaces had either been sold off or destroyed by water and a lack of maintenance. In addition, when the hotel was originally designed in 1900, many conveniences expected in a

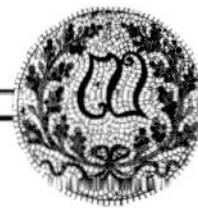

Carol M. Highsmith

Removing a Cornice Detail

luxury hotel today had not been invented and were not built into the hotel. The hotel rooms were also not laid out in the most efficient manner.

The restoration requirements of the public were met with some compromise and a great deal of careful research as well as the talents of some specialized artisans. Originally, the ballrooms of the Willard were placed in the mansard roof on the top floor. These grand rooms took their form from the thirty foot, barrel-vaulted shape of the roof and captured, through oversized windows, some of the most dramatic vistas of the City. Unfortunately, due to the same concerns expressed by the Fire Marshall in 1946 when he turned down the night club proposal, it was not practical or safe to attempt to accommodate large crowds at the top of the hotel. With some reluctance, the Park Service and PADC allowed the ballroom to be moved to the basement of the complex and the old ballroom space to the filled with guest rooms.

Although 95% of the interior of the hotel would eventually be removed because of its poor condition, all of the ground floor spaces except for the rooms on the west side of Peacock Alley were meticulously restored requiring extensive work and careful reproduction of the elements which had been destroyed or lost.

The lobby, the Willard Room, Crystal Room, Round Robin Bar, Ladies Lounge, F Street Lobby and Peacock Alley were all recreated to the detail of their original splendor. In order to accomplish this, a team was put together including members of the architect's staff, a talented Greek craftsman named John Barianos and the interior design talents of Tom Lee, Ltd. of New York. This group went painstakingly through the hotel, locating portions of original woodwork and plaster detail which were intact, scraping through as many as sixteen layers of paint to find original colors, uncovering columns and the original tile floor and searching out bits and pieces of fabric which could have been original decoration.

The research work in the hotel was supplemented by historical research to locate written descriptions of the hotel when it was opened in 1901, photographs of the original public

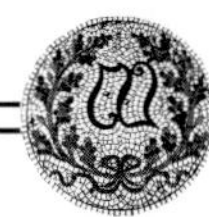

spaces, which showed considerable detail but not color, and people who could recall the hotel in its heyday. This research coupled with the on site investigations enabled the design team to develop an accurate picture of the original finish detailing of the public spaces.

Having determined the detail to which the hotel should be restored, the next task was to actually accomplish the work. John Barianos had the job of restoring the floors, columns and ceiling details. Thirty-five varieties of marble had been used in the Willard which had been obtained world-wide. He was told that the marble for the tile floor was no longer available, so he spent a month looking through old mines in the hills around Sienna, Italy until he found one with the color stone he needed. There are over 7,000 square feet of marble floors on the ground level made up of 3/4 inch marble squares. The job of restoring this floor was akin to completing a jigsaw puzzle with over one million pieces. Each square was lifted out, cleaned and shaped as necessary and replaced in a new cement base.

Barianos examined the scagliola columns in the public rooms, the decorative plaster, and the woodwork and identified sections that could be used as molds and forms for the replication required to restore these grand spaces. Where sections of plaster, cornice work and other elaborate detailing were found intact, new molds were made by brushing latex on the old form in sixteen or seventeen layers until a form evolved with enough strength, yet flexibility, to mold identical sections. The original interior columns in the lobby and the Crystal and Willard rooms had been made out of scagliola instead of marble, a cost saving technique at the turn of the century. Scagliola is plaster which has been painted to look like marble. This work was restored by replicating the process by which the columns

Carol M. Highsmith

Finishing Scagliola

were originally made. A rough layer of plaster was formed in the shape of the column around each structural steel member. On this was applied a fine layer of plaster onto which silk thread had been laid. The correct colors for the column were then rubbed into the plaster and the silk threads pulled through to achieve the marblized affect of the finished work.

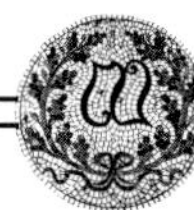

The Willard Room–Early Restoration

The oak paneling in the Willard rooms was restored and missing or destroyed pieces were replaced with identical woodwork copied from existing pieces. The upper levels of the room, which are actually plaster designed to look like the wood, have been restored. Chandeliers and sconces have been reproduced in brass and bronze cast from new forms based on photographic records of the original fixtures.

Physical construction itself presented significant problems. The original building was a steel frame structure with terra cotta tile used as a base for the floors and for solid interior partitions. While an improvement over previous building systems, the tile was brittle and difficult to work with. When the plumbers were installing the twelve miles of new pipe required to service the new hotel they had to pull out the old pipe required to service the new hotel as well as the old pipe sleeves in the floor. When this was attempted, however, the surrounding tile fractured. The floors presented a similar problem; the terra cotta was too brittle to sustain the weight of the new service elements of the building. Therefore, the engineers had to design a system to transfer the weight of the new improvements onto the steel frame.

In the public spaces there was the additional problem of having to pass pipes and conduits over the decorative ceilings as well as providing for a new sprinkler system. To solve this

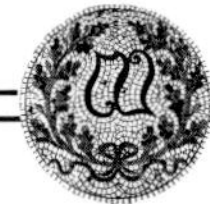

Carol M. Highsmith

The Willard Room–Mid Restoration

problem, a raised floor was built approximately twenty inches above the existing second floor allowing space to run pipes and drains and providing the workmen space to install electrical fixtures and sprinkler heads.

The roof provided a similar challenge. Because of its barrel shape, its terra cotta underlayment and the deteriorated condition of the slate, it would not bear the weight required to replace it. Supported from girders on the ninth floor, a system of interlocking scaffolding was used to span the roof without touching it. From this structure, workmen replaced the old slate and installed the new in the same manner it was originally installed in 1901. The ornamental metalwork on the roof was lifted out through the scaffolding by hand, repaired and then put back in place through the metal grid.

In order to provide for a more efficient guest room layout, one other substantial physical change was made. The original hotel plan had the guestrooms laid out parallel to Fourteenth Street. This configuration tended to reduce the number of rooms which could be provided on the site. A new plan was drawn calling for the rooms to be turned 90 degrees, thus running perpendicular to Fourteenth Street and the main corridor of the hotel. This was accomplished by removing the interior wall of the hotel facing the alley and by widening the building by one structural bay. This permitted the architects to provide for nearly four hundred rooms while freeing up the land in the middle of the block for the office building.

For the new portion of the project, the architectural objective was a real challenge to the designers. The scheme which needed to be implemented was a wing cascading to Pennsylvania Avenue from F Street in four steps. The new materials were to be architectural, cast concrete, a counterpoint to the

Carol M. Highsmith

limestone base of the old structure, a light brick shaded slightly off the Willard brick color, to separate the new from the old, and a metal mansard roof complementing the grand French style of the hotel's slate mansard roof. Balconies, dormers and bulls eye windows in the new addition have been created out of cast stone as reflections of the highly ornamented detail of the hotel. To enhance the public space of the terraced courtyard extending from F Street to the Avenue, three grand fountains have been installed, visually adding a sense of distinction to

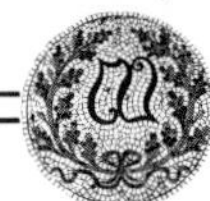

Carol M. Highsmith

Installing a Cornice

Carol M. Highsmith

Finishing Touches

the exterior promenade, and introducing the sound of water to this urban setting. To bridge the new and the old, making the connection to the two buildings and announcing the physical entrance to the office building lobby, a marble baldachino, or foyer, was constructed in the same style as the entry porticoes to the Willard and the courtyard.

One of the most difficult tasks was to recreate the interior finish for the public spaces in the hotel; the lobby, Peacock Alley, the Crystal and Willard Rooms, the Round Robin Bar and the Ladies Lounge, the F Street entrance and the oval suites at the corner of Pennsylvania Avenue and Fourteenth Street. The objective was to restore the original decor and to achieve a result that would be suited to present day tastes. To undertake the task of restoration, with the challenge of furnishing the hotel, Tom Lee, Ltd. of New York, was selected, and the task has been completed with the finest sense of history and elegance.

Research work on the hotel had produced a palet of colors which were used in the public rooms, and photographs taken by Frances Benjamin Johnston had documented much of the

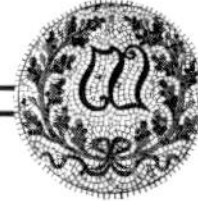

Installing a State Seal in the Lobby

detail of the hotel furnishings. What the designers discovered, however, was that the colors were too harsh for modern tastes. In order to create a result that would meet the restoration requirements of the Park Service and demands of a modern public, the designers softened the tone of the colors and with the effective use of modern day lighting, which is brighter than that used in 1901, created a spectacular overall effect.

Many segments simply had to be created from the best information available. Photographs revealed the original design of some of the carpets but not the coloring. Using newspaper mention of the color and the paint color scheme, a nine color carpet was designed and then specially woven in Warwick, England for the new lobby.

The original 48 state seals which had been in the coffered lobby ceiling were located, but they were so badly damaged that copies had to be made and reinstalled. Seals for Alaska and Hawaii have also been produced, awaiting only the selection of a location compatible with the historic design. Chandaliers have been recreated from photographs, and in the case of the lobby, by the firm that made the original fixtures eighty five years ago.

Furnishing the hotel, both public areas and guestrooms, proved to be a special challenge. The public spaces have been furnished in the style of their turn-of-the-century victorian elegance with plush, over-stuffed period reproductions. Of the 394 hotel rooms, there are 65 suites and 140 different room layouts providing a challenge for the development of consistent design themes. The Presidential suite has been recreated in Empire style with bright colors and $120,000 in antiques from Sothebys as well as period reproductions. Other suites, such as the Lincoln, Federal and Capital, have been furnished in Empire as well as Federal style. The typical guestrooms have been furnished in two basic styles of decor; one, light with white furniture and French floral fabrics reminiscent of a Newport summer cottage, and the other, more masculine, with the use of a brown color palette and carved fruitwood furniture. All rooms are outfitted with the latest in luxury hotel room conveniences and the overall result, from the grand ballroom in the basement to the honeymoon suite tucked away in the cupola at the very top of the hotel, is a hotel of unsurpassed elegance.

At long last, after nearly three years of construction and painstaking restoration, in the summer of 1986, the crown jewel of Pennsylvania Avenue was primed for rebirth. Closed

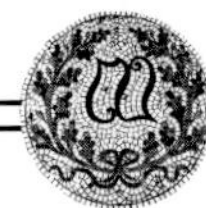

Carol M. Highsmith

The Completed Project

Harry Naltchayan, The Washington Post

Napier Gala–1986

for over eighteen years, the hotel was opened to the public on August 20, 1986 in much the same way as in 1901. The doors were swung wide and the public was invited in to view the masterful work. As chance would have it, the hotel had two of its first visitors on the preceeding evening. Carol Channing and Mary Martin were starring in a performance of "Legends" nearby at the National Theatre when their performance was interrupted by a bomb scare. The ladies knocked on the Willard front door looking for a place of safety and were gladly let in.

There were two small celebrations on this special day. Mr. and Mrs. Tom Moore were the first to sign the register when the Willard's doors reopened. The Moores had visited Washington back in 1968 and had registered at the Willard on the recommendation of their Congressman, George Bush. As it turned out, the Moores were the last guests to check out of the hotel, and the management appropriately invited them to be the first guests to check in. Vice President Bush sent the Moores a new congratulatory letter to memorialize the happy occasion.

Just off the lobby, in the Round Robin bar, a group of retired Board members of the National Press Club gathered to reopen the bar. They had been there on that fateful closing day in 1968 and drank the last round little knowing that their salute to a passing tradition had been premature.

With that beautiful and historic day in August, the Willard came alive and was given back to the City and the people that loved it. Hundreds of people waited outside the hotel doors just for the chance to enter and walk once again down Peacock Alley. People strolled down the corridors recalling fond memories. A group of Mennonite friends posed for pictures in the Crystal Room, in striking contrast to the lavishness of the room, but also strangely reminiscent of the affection stored up in those hallowed walls.

The public visits of August were succeeded by a series of formal events during the third week of September. On Monday, September 20, a ribbon-cutting ceremony was held with officials representing all of the organizations responsible for saving the hotel and restoring it as well as a cast of Willard heirs. On Tuesday evening, a special dinner was held in honor of Ronald Reagan as a fund raiser for his alma mater, Eureka College. Reagan fondly recalled his days as one of Eureka's Golden Tornadoes and as a dishwasher in the girl's dormitory. There may have been a little mist in his eyes when he was presented, after all these years, with his class ring.

The week's events climaxed with a grand party Wednesday evening reminiscent of the Napier Ball of 1859. That evening, the entire hotel was turned over to celebration and guests feasted and danced til the early hours of morning.

Airs and speeches have faded away, but not so the Willard. It is renewed again, physically and in spirit. The parade is passing down Peacock Alley. The hotel once again plays host to Presidents. The Willard family, its heritage intertwined with the hotel, once again owns a part of this history. Most of all, the Willard is back, and with it a special place in the hearts and minds of everyone who has walked these popular corridors and with a new sense of hope for another century of grand hospitality.

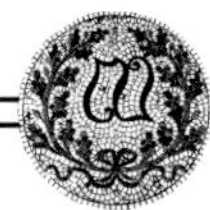

BIBLIOGRAPHY

Barnum, P.T. *Barnum's Own Story: Autobiography of P.T. Barnum,* New York: Viking Press, 1927.

Dickens, Charles. *America Notes* (Reprint), New York: St. Martin's Press.

Eskew, Garnett Laidlaw. *Willard's of Washington,* New York: Coward-McCann, Inc., 1954.

Green, Constance McLaughlin. *Washington Village and Capitol, 1800–1878,* Princeton, New Jersey: Princeton University Press, 1962.

Green, Constance McLaughlin. *Washington Capital City, 1879–1950, Princeton, New Jersey: Princeton University Press, 1963.*

Hawthorne, Nathaniel. "Chiefly About War Matters," Atlantic Monthly, July, 1862.

Kalb, Phyllis. "The Willard—A Historical Romance," Research Paper, prepared for the Oliver T. Carr Company, 1985.

Kiplinger, W.M. *Washington Is Like That,* New York: Harper & Brothers Publishers, 1942.

Leech, Margaret. *Reveille in Washington, 1860–1865,* New York: Harper & Brothers, 1941.

Leup, Francis E., and Lester G. Hornby. *Walks About Washington,* Boston: Little, Brown and Company, 1915.

Montgomery, Dean R. "The Willard Hotels of Washington, D.C., 1847–1968," Records of the Columbia Historical Society, Washington, D.C., 1966–1968.

Paine, Albert Bigelow. *Mark Twain: A Biography,* New York: Washington, D.C., 1969.

Pepper, Charles M. *Every-Day Life in Washington,* New York: The Christian Herald, 1900.

Proctor, John Claggett. *Proctor's Washington and Environs,* (Written for the *Washington Sunday Star,* 1928–1949), 1949.

Proctor, John Claggett. *Washington Past and Present,* New York: Lewis Historical Publishing Company, 1930.

Report of the President's Council on Pennsylvania Avenue, *Pennsylvania Avenue,* U.S. Government Printing Office, 1964.

Richards, Julia E. and Maud Howe Elliott. *Julia Ward Howe. 1819–1910,* Cambridge: Houghton Griffin Co., The Riverside Press, 1925.

Washington Board of Trade. *The Book of Washington,* Washington, D.C., 1930.

Whitman, Walt. "Memoranda During The War," 1875.

Willard, Henry K. "Henry Augustus Willard: His Life and Times," Records of the Columbia Historical Society, Washington, D.C., 1917.

Willard, Joseph C. Personal Diary, 1880.

ADDITIONAL REFERENCES

Joseph C. Willard vs. Benjamin O. Tayloe, 75 US. 557-574, 1867.

Joseph C. Willard vs. Henry K. Willard, Supreme Court of the United States, October Term, 1891, No. 318.

United States Court of Claims, 548 F.2d. 939.

National Register of Historic Places Nomination, Tanya Beauchamp, NCPC, 1979.

The Willard Family Papers, Manuscript Division, Library of Congress.

"The Willard Hotel Feasibility Study," prepared by The Oliver T. Carr Company, October 1, 1974.

Wilard Guidebook, O.G. Staples, Ca. 1880.

Back Issues
Harper's Weekly.
The Daily National Intelligencer.
The National Geographic.
The Vermonter.
The Washington Post.
The Washington Star.
The Washington Times-Herald.

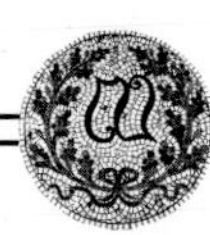